To Marisa, Casey and Phillipa. The girls in my life. And thanks to
Imogen for her work and effort.
Philip Sparrowhawk – August 2003

Martin Knight would like to dedicate this book
to Harry Knight (1920–2003)

*For a variety of legal and emotional reasons, some of
the names in this book have been changed.
In other cases, my memory has failed me – I have problems
remembering all my names, let alone others.

Phil Sparrowhawk
with Martin King and Martin Knight

GRASS

MAINSTREAM
PUBLISHING
EDINBURGH AND LONDON

This edition 2004

First published in Great Britain in 2003 by
MAINSTREAM PUBLISHING (EDINBURGH) LTD
7 Albany Street
Edinburgh EH1 3UG

ISBN 1 84018 892 8

A catalogue record for this book is available from the British Library

Typeset in Apollo and Billboard

Printed in Great Britain by
Cox & Wyman Ltd

CONTENTS

FOREWORD BY HOWARD MARKS

It would be imprudent to say for how long the dope smuggling partnership Phil Sparrowhawk and I shared lasted, but during the time it did, we visited several dozen countries together, smuggled countless tons of Thai marijuana and a few tons of hashish, and made millions of pounds. I have never known him smoke a joint. And we are still the best of friends.

Phil's mood, temperament and demeanour never alter. His appearance is constantly nondescript (ideal for a man in our line of business). One could never tell whether Phil was on his tenth million or down to his last pound note. He was a working-class boy, equally fired by the desire to acquire wealth as the quest for adventure. If Phil had been born a century earlier, he would have read the *Boy's Own* paper and become a big-game hunter, exploring far-flung lands in his spare time.

During 1974, I skipped bail and became a fugitive. Disappearing itself is quite simple: one could jog in Iraq or do business in Afghanistan (a task I later entrusted to Phil). If cheating mortality is neither permitted nor desired, one could take the hardcore option of checking into any Third World prison (also experienced by Phil). Forget heterosexuality, good nosh, and breathtaking vistas; but there's plenty of dope, libraries and gymnasiums. Most people, however, prefer freedom.

The two most important parameters relating to successful disappearance are position and appearance. At constantly new locations where one is unknown, appearance is irrelevant. On the other hand, if one's appearance is constantly changing, it doesn't matter where one is. Playing safe, I decided to change my appearance and travel. I rented a bedsit, stayed inside, either shaved or grew a moustache and beard, adopted a radically new hairstyle, and varied the takeaway diet. Bedsits were boring, so I filled idle moments by applying to the DVLC in Swansea for a few provisional driving licences. I used any names that came to mind and once obtained one in the name of Elvis Presley. The Swansea computer didn't bat an eyelid; it didn't remember the 1950s. I got loads of junk mail in different names. I joined cheesy clubs and got bits of plastic that looked like credit cards. I got real. I got a life. In fact, I got a few lives and supplemented them with different clothes, walking sticks, crutches, eye-patches, scars, wigs, shades, wheelchairs and spectacles. I then took driving tests with the provisional licences and got Post Office Savings accounts with full licences as identification, and with those I got bank accounts. But passports remained elusive. My first meeting with Phil arose out of this need for false identity: a common acquaintance had suggested he could be useful.

Various passports are available in the criminal marketplace, but, ideally, one wants a passport actually issued by one of the passport offices (so that it withstands today's sophisticated border checks) and one wants as few people as possible to know the name (so friends can't grass you up). There are plenty of people, for example certified lunatics and the terminally ill, who can't travel abroad. There are others who have no intention of visiting different countries because they don't trust foreign beer. Filling in an application form with the appropriate details was easy. The tricky bit was getting it countersigned by someone who existed. It seemed much easier to get it countersigned by someone who didn't exist by renting another bedsit in another name and become a referee. But there are only so many rooms one can rent. I needed someone who could give me an address that could be anyone's and answer the phone as whoever I chose. (The only check the Passport Office was ever likely to make was to telephone the referee and ask if he'd countersigned the application and photograph.) I asked Phil if he could help. He said he would. The rest is his story.

I found *Grass* a delight to read. Some of our combined history I had forgotten, and much of Phil's life before and after our partnership was unknown to me. Phil's extraordinary pragmatism and relaxed attitude to his circumstances and surroundings shine and reveal themselves throughout his book. Only he could spend years in a Thai prison and actually enjoy the experience. Sit down, skin-up, and read.

Howard Marks,
Spain
August 2003

Part One

THE END

SPACE INVADERS
BANGKOK, THAILAND

JULY 1988

I've tried not to count my blessings ever since. It's asking for trouble. I know I was feeling good that morning because I remember every tiny detail of the entire day; for reasons that will become clear it has etched itself in my memory. The sun was already up and out as I walked out of my door and hopped up into my red Suzuki Jeep. Before I pulled away I glanced over at my house and bathed momentarily in a feeling of wellbeing. I was a successful businessman. Inside, still asleep, were my lovely Thai girlfriend and our wonderful young daughter; I had plenty of money in the bank and enjoyed a jet-setting lifestyle I would never have dreamt of in my younger days. Actually, I did dream about it, that's why I followed the path I did, but I suppose I never really believed I'd get there.

When I turned on the ignition, the radio came on and the plummy but comforting voice of the BBC World Service newsreader floated around the car. My general sense of contentment and absolute control of my destiny increased. Mrs Thatcher was riding high in the opinion polls; she had been in power nearly a decade now and I was hoping for another ten years. Since the retaking of the Falkland Islands a few years earlier she had re-established the perception of Britain as a world power. Maggie was widely believed to be pulling Ronald Reagan's strings and he in turn was forcing President Gorbachev of Russia to slowly disarm. The Cold War was thawing, the world was becoming a safer place and suddenly there was an illusion that the Brits were running the show again. For someone in my line of work this could only be for the good. Being British gave you a degree of automatic respect in foreign parts and you were less likely to be suspected of being up to any nonsense.

When the radio reporters got on to the subject of what appeared to be the final days of the Iran–Iraq war (it seemed to be drawing to a close only because they were running out of people to kill on either side), I switched over to an American radio station and drummed my fingers on the steering wheel along to Grace Slick singing 'Nothing's Gonna Stop Us Now'. 'Her band,' the DJ said, 'is called Starship.' I remembered it as Jefferson Airplane, but there you go, you've got to move with the times. The song summed up my mood perfectly.

I joined the flow of traffic from my suburb into the centre of Bangkok and proceeded at a snail's pace. Business commuters jockeyed for scarce road space with open-backed Toyota trucks and tuk-tuks full of smiling Thais off to work on the building sites. By now, and as usual, traffic was virtually at a standstill, so when I saw two men on motorbikes stationary behind me, I knew I was being followed. If not, they could and would have weaved and squeezed in and out of the cars to beat the jam. I was not too alarmed or surprised at this, however, as a business associate had warned me a few days before that officers from the US Drugs Enforcement Agency (DEA) were closing in and that I should be extremely careful.

The DEA, and one US Government agent in particular, had got it into their heads that the entire world's ills were mainly the fault of a man called Howard Marks, who they knew had been moving cannabis around the globe for many years. Although he was British, Welsh to be precise, he was, I suppose, America's most wanted in their 'fight against drugs'. Howard famously had been acquitted by an Old Bailey jury in 1981 of drug trafficking and had put a number of noses out of joint when he continued to ply his trade, in an open and brash fashion, in the eyes of the authorities at least.

I had been doing business with Howard for many years. A decade earlier, I had worked for him, but nowadays he was simply one of my many partners, customers and business associates. While I knew that the DEA were sniffing around me, I didn't realise at the time that my long association with Howard had made me second only to him on the long list of DEA targets.

I had heard some weeks before from one of my Thai contacts that questions were being asked about me by the Americans and that I was likely to be arrested by the Thai police. I was led to believe this would be more to show willing than anything else. You have to realise that the Thai race does not share the abhorrence the Western world affects over soft drugs. Grass grows naturally, like hops, on their land and until the sex industry developed, it was the main export underpinning their economy. But when the world's superpowers tell you the flow of these substances has to stop, you have to play their game. Especially if they are pumping billions of dollars into your economy.

I hadn't been particularly concerned about the interest being shown in my affairs, as I had large amounts of money and lived in a country where money not only spoke, it positively hollered. I believed that my connections in high places in Thailand were sufficiently influential to protect me. I had someone on the inside at the DEA who was feeding me the information I needed to keep one step ahead of them, so I had the confidence of a man who had been getting away with it all his life. Finally, despite the risks, I was determined to complete the transaction I was working on — exporting five tons of grass into Amsterdam for shipment on to Australia — before I started worrying about the DEA, the CIA, New Scotland Yard, or anyone else. I had decided that this deal would be my last and I would focus entirely on my legitimate interests. Hence my 'end of term' mood.

The bike riders clearly weren't fully alert yet because I swung a left without indicating and before they clocked it I had chucked a right and lost them. I sighed and continued along a back-road route to the small hotel I had previously checked into. I always used a small hotel when I was in the middle of a deal: using their phone was safer than using any of mine. It was only a tenner a night – although, of course, I had no use for it at night – and I got a decent room and some privacy. My real office was just around the corner in an old-style Thai house, and from there I publicly ran my legitimate food export business and, up until recently, my popular and respectable massage parlour, which was a concession in the Hyatt Central Hotel.

When I got back on to the Sukhumvit Road, unfortunately I ran straight into the motorcyclists and this time they were so close that I could see their faces. They were Thais though, not Westerners, and that made me feel a little easier. Nevertheless, I pulled into the car park of the Ambassador Hotel, got out of the car and left my briefcase on the back seat. The briefcase contained all the papers and necessary documentation pertaining to the Amsterdam deal and I thought it safer to leave it there. Without looking back, I walked through the main entrance of the Ambassador and straight out the back entrance, and then took off to the hotel I was really using. I couldn't see if the men were following me.

In the hotel, Uncle Joe, an Australian man in his 50s with the swarthy tanned features of a ship's captain, was waiting for me outside his room. I was supplying Joe with the Thai grass he would be importing into Australia via Holland. Although geographically Thailand was far closer to Australia than Holland, it was still cheaper and smoother for me to send it to Amsterdam and for Joe to get it shipped to Oz from there. The Dutch were more laid back about this type of thing and demanded far less in bribes.

'I think I'm being followed, Uncle,' I said and started to tell Joe about the morning's events. I had already told him about the arrest tip-off. Joe scratched his beard. He was not a man to panic – he'd been in this line of business for years and these days didn't touch a deal of less than five tons. That would fetch around A$25 million on the streets of Sydney. Joe organised the private yachts that brought the grass into his country and the initial onward distribution.

'Your brother called from England,' he said. 'He seemed worried about something.'

I immediately phoned Tony and was taken aback to hear that I *had* been arrested. He read out a small item from that day's *Daily Telegraph* – DRUGS BARON UNDER ARREST – 'Philip Sparrowhawk, an Englishman, has been arrested in Bangkok, Thailand, by the US Drugs Enforcement Agency on suspicion of drugs trafficking offences.'

Fuck me, I had heard of newspapers making things up but this was a bit close to home. I knew now I was definitely going to be arrested. The DEA's press office had merely sent out their press release a few hours too early. Confident or what?

Joe and I decided to make ourselves scarce. We left the room and went downstairs to the foyer, where he turned right and I turned left. Before I could register that there were more people in the lobby area than normal, I was pounced on and dragged to the floor. My hands were cuffed behind my back and then I was lifted to my feet. 'What room have you just come from?' screamed an American voice.

Of course they were DEA, all in their black suits and black ties. They rugby tackled Joe to the floor when he made the mistake of hesitating for a second after I was jumped. They then lifted him up and ran with him up to his room, where they quickly found a kilo of grass that I had taken to him two days earlier as a sample. Joe was carted off and I was grabbed by the neck and pushed into the back of a Toyota car. There was really no need for any of the rough stuff, as I offered no resistance, but adrenalin was clearly running high among the Yanks. We made a short car journey to the 'secret' DEA headquarters, which were less than 100 yards from my office. Some secret HQ: I knew every car, motorbike and face that had been going in and out of there for the previous three years.

As the DEA got me out of their motor they were just yelling and shouting. I had no idea I had fucked so many mothers or sucked so many cocks. The Thai police, who were in on the operation and may well have been the motorbike men, kept shouting at me 'Where is your car, where is your car?'

'I can't remember,' I lied.

The commotion attracted a crowd. A crowd gathers in Bangkok if someone farts loudly, but they especially enjoy road accidents and shootings. They even have a magazine on general sale dedicated to real murders and fatal accidents with colour pictures of the aftermath of such gory incidents. If their photographers miss the action, they re-enact the scene with actors and actresses using tomato sauce. I kid you not.

Inside the DEA building I was photographed again and again. Each time, I shook my head to try and send my glasses flying and each time they pushed them back on my face. They had fallen for it – I wanted them to have pictures with glasses on and not off. Under the identity I was using at the time – that of an Irishman named Daniel Hamrogue – I always wore glasses. Under previous identities, and mainly because I hadn't needed them so much when I was younger, I didn't. The DEA were interested in an Englishman called Philip Sparrowhawk who didn't always wear glasses.

'Where's the briefcase?'

That was a relief: the fact they were asking meant they had not found my car yet. All the evidence, on the Holland deal at least, was in that briefcase. But they did know about the briefcase. When they kept on and on, I told them to ask the two boys who had been following me.

'How did you know you were being followed? If you knew you were being followed why did you still go to meet your friend?'

'I didn't go to meet anyone. I didn't worry about being followed because I have done nothing wrong.' I was beginning to believe my own protestations of innocence.

After this first round of questions they put me back in their car and drove me out to my house. It was not a large house, more like the Thai equivalent of a Wimpey starter home; it was terraced and I had paid the Thai equivalent of around £30,000 for it. In my line of business, flouting your wealth is rather stupid.

Luckily the Thais knocked on the door before the Americans could kick it off its hinges and storm in, guns drawn. I tried to reassure my girlfriend as drawers were upturned and my papers stuffed into bags. They found phone numbers and other bits and pieces, but there was nothing there of any value to them. Finally they gave up and we headed back to DEA headquarters, where I was questioned and shouted at all over again. It was now seven o'clock in the evening and I had been arrested at around ten in the morning. My hands were still cuffed behind me and I had not had a drink, anything to eat or a shit or piss all day. The police now told me that Uncle Joe was already banged up in Klong Prem Central Prison, the small piece of grass found in his room being enough to put him in there immediately.

They were getting nowhere fast with me so we went off on another car ride, this time past the British and American embassies to the Immigration Holding Centre on Satorn Road. I had heard about this place but had never before had the pleasure of visiting it. I was handed over to the Thai authorities and the Americans drove off into the night.

'You Philip Sparrowhawk,' the guard on the desk informed me.

'No, me Daniel Hamrogue,' I replied, sticking with my current identity and the name on the Irish passport I had been using. The Americans wanted Philip Sparrowhawk and had obviously told them who I was. Frankly, the Thais didn't give a shit.

'Why are our American friends so angry with you, Daniel?' The guard was miffed that the Yanks had brought someone in for processing at this time of night. His television flickered away in the corner of his office, competing sound-wise with the hum of the air-conditioning unit. Next to the television was his bed. He had obviously been sleeping in it before my arrival.

I was passed on to another guard, open-shirted and sweating heavily, who led me upstairs. 'Have you been arrested at the airport?' he asked.

At the top of the stairs there were two rooms separated by a narrow landing. These rooms or cells measured about forty feet by sixteen feet. They were concrete up to about four and a half feet and then bars ran the rest of the way to the ceiling. The guard opened the wooden door and shoved me into a sea of bodies. These were the people who *had* been arrested at the airport.

The first thing that hit me was the stench – a sickly cocktail of urine, sweat and shit – and as I looked down I could see the room was full of bodies, people trying to sleep. When I later counted, there were 160 people crammed into that cell and whilst there was slightly more room when everyone stood up, when it was lay-down time the crush was unimaginable. There is a Marx Brothers film where scores of people cram into a tiny room. It was like that but this was no comedy. Dim light came from two fluorescent tubes that were clogged with dead flies and mosquitoes and by this I could see some faces. One was a black face, looking at me as I stood by the door dumbstruck and hesitant; he was sitting cross-legged with his back against the wall and he beckoned me over. I trod carefully, on tiptoes, my feet finding the odd square inch of concrete floor among the legs, arms, heads and torsos, and crossed the room towards him.

From this squatting vantage point next to my black friend I could survey the room. There were no chairs, no beds, no windows, no nothing. A hole in the concrete floor on the other side of the room was obviously a toilet and there was a smidgen of space around it – not to spare anyone's modesty but because sleeping or standing right next to it would have killed anyone within hours, from the smell alone. Nearby was a cold tap attached to a rusty old pipe. The vast majority of the prisoners, on first glance at least, appeared to be Asian – Burmese, Chinese, Vietnamese, Pakistani and Indian. My neighbour spoke some English and he briefly told me he was a Ghanaian and had been arrested for entering the country with an incorrect visa. That was six months ago. He then fell silent to allow me to digest my new situation.

Not until you have been deprived of it do you realise how important space is to you. In the hierarchy of things you need to survive, it ranks way above sex and not far below food and drink. Think of how claustrophobic you feel when standing on a packed tube train: the doors open and there is clearly no room, but a few more idiots crush in and you are tilting your neck back to breathe in the air as the mackintoshes and briefcases press up against you. Think of enduring that, not for the few minutes between Bank and Waterloo stations, but all the fucking time. Think of the hottest day of the year in England. Think of all those commuters near naked and sweating profusely. Think of all those people deciding to lie down on the floor and try to sleep. Think then of the space in the corner where the doors would open being used for people to go to the toilet. Think of the proximity. Think of the smell. Mind the doors. You're about halfway there now.

I didn't sleep that first night. There were a hundred things racing around my mind and I didn't dare. I feared for my life in that room. But at that point I still saw my predicament as a mere hiccup in this eventful life of mine.

At about six in the morning, arms and legs started to unfold, bollocks were scratched and the hole in the ground became busy as bladders and bowels were emptied. There was a civilised shuffling for space as the cell adjusted to the incremental room now nearly everyone was standing. Tied around and hanging from the bars were the belongings of people who had been apprehended at the airport. The duty-free bags were the giveaway. Most people were dressed in underwear or sarongs and conversations broke out in various Asian dialects. A kettle was lit and soon the air became thick with cigarette smoke.

'Be careful of the Chinese,' whispered the Ghanaian, 'they are the traders in here. If you have money they will sell you anything: tea, bottled water, cigarettes, a knife for protection, weed, smack.'

'What? You can get smack in here?'

'This is Thailand. If you have the money, you can get anything in here.'

At eight o'clock a guard appeared with stacks of metal trays containing portions of rice and cabbage soup. A Cambodian who had become an orderly on account of his two and a half years in this room dished them out, holding a baseball bat just in case there was a rush or some outbreak of disorder at feeding time. This was unlikely, however, as the place was so overcrowded that rushing or even throwing a punch was not really an option. After the meal was finished, the trays were all passed across the room to the tap where they were washed and stacked up again for the guard to take away.

I spotted a white face among the crowd and threaded my way over to speak to him. He was German and had been in prison in Thailand for three years for passing dodgy travellers' cheques. He had served his time and had been transferred to the Immigration Centre pending his flight home. That was six weeks ago. He didn't have the money for a ticket and until he got that in from somewhere he was going nowhere. He told me that the guy next to him had been in for just over two years because he didn't have the money – the equivalent of about £20 – to pay a fine for having a visa that was 18 days out of date. It was rapidly becoming obvious that the holding centre served no other purpose than to raise money for the holding centre itself, or at least the guards who ran it. There was no question of this being about the containment of undesirables or the gathering of information. As I soon discovered, the only release from here was procured by death or money. I had plenty of the latter, so I was looking forward to getting this little mess straightened out quickly.

After a couple of days my girlfriend tracked me down, although she got no help from the DEA or the Thai police, and she immediately arranged for me to have access to some cash. The first thing I bought was bottled water from the guards; my thirst had become such that I had almost succumbed to drinking from the rusty old tap. I also paid to use a toilet. I had not had a shit now for four or five days, as I could not bring myself to unload in front of all these people. Nowadays TV programmes such as *An Audience with Ken Dodd* or some other celebrity are popular; I was determined not to stage *An Audience with Phil Sparrowhawk's Arsehole*. Getting the shits in this place could also have been fatal. I gave my girlfriend some instructions and hoped the wheels would now be turning to get me out and home.

Before I had been in a week, I witnessed my first suicide. I hadn't noticed the man before. He was 30 feet away. I think he was Vietnamese – one of the so-called boat people. He was an economic refugee, not a criminal, and even if he had committed some crime it would have been out of desperation not greed. It was late evening and the first thing I noticed was the sound of him tearing his T-shirt into strips and tying the strips together. My immediate thought was that he was going to hang himself but as no one said a word or even gave him a second glance, I figured he must be doing something else. Perhaps he was one of those obsessive-compulsive people who tear bits of paper up all day. Before I could fully grasp what was going on he had tied his 'rope' around the bars and was climbing on the shoulders of the two people either side of him. One of these men was conducting a whispered conversation with the man next to him. The other pulled on a cigarette in a totally detached fashion. I went to move towards them, hardly believing what I was seeing, but the Ghanaian put his hand on my arm and shook his head firmly. The man jumped off his neighbours' shoulders and they moved away, leaving a space around the poor fellow who was now hanging, jerking and spluttering. No one really seemed to be looking. I think they were being polite. This was his private moment. When I asked why no one was cutting him down, I was told that if they did they would leave themselves open to being accused of some sort of foul play. The guards would cut him down in the morning. I soon realised why a space was left below his hanging body. During the night I could see and hear the shit and piss dripping to the floor from the legs of his shorts.

The suicide upset me but didn't seem to perturb anyone else, not even the other Vietnamese who must have known this man. I realised that they must all have become hardened to it, as suicides were commonplace. It was one of the few options open to you in here (the others were to anaesthetise yourself with drugs or go mad) and death was generally an occupational hazard for refugees in this part of the world.

The next day, routine had been resumed and the suicide forgotten, and, with a few shuffles of feet and bottoms, his space had been claimed. A young life had ended with less impact than if a light bulb had popped in a family sitting room in Maidstone. I doubt if the man had a birth certificate. I'm sure he didn't get a death certificate. He would not have been travelling on his real name. But someone, somewhere must have known him, must have loved, held and nurtured him. I doubted if they would ever get to know of his fate.

Although the guards didn't fully enter the room to deposit the food, which came again (same menu) at four in the afternoon, they were forever in and out bringing in the various goodies that the inmates had ordered. Newspapers and books were in demand, as were sweets and other simple pleasures. The only time I saw the guards dish out violence was to prisoners who had not paid for their orders. This could be vicious, but all they really wanted to do was earn and have a quiet life – the Thais were never into violence for violence's sake.

My girlfriend's visits had made my life more tolerable almost immediately. The guards viewed me as a possible source of income as opposed to a chore and my status among the prisoners was immediately elevated. After my girlfriend dropped the Baht equivalent of £1,000 on them, the guards became positively warm towards me and I was given some blankets and a prized space up against the wall. I knew enough Thai to know that they were also warning other inmates to treat me well. One day I had a craving for Kentucky Fried Chicken, actually I had a craving for anything non-soup or rice-based, but knew if my girlfriend brought me one in I was risking a riot. So I told her to bring 40 boxes, which fed just about everyone something and raised my standing further. We didn't share any with the Chinese, as they'd only sell it on. A few days later we did the same with pizza. I bought water, sweets, newspapers and books, and distributed them as widely as I could. The guards loved me and so did everyone else. Within a couple of weeks I was being treated like a king. Of course, this had a downside, which was that the guards were probably not too keen for me to move on. I asked on several occasions when I was going to be let out but they just said nothing or 'Soon, soon.' I had no visits from the British Embassy but I couldn't really complain about that too much when I was insisting to anyone who enquired that I was Irish.

The Ghanaian became my closest friend in the centre and I called him James, as in James Garner (Ghana), the Hollywood actor. This was easier for me to remember than his real name. I was able to direct some financial assistance on the outside to his visa problem and soon he was released. He was very grateful and, although I was pleased to be able to help at least one of the wretched people in there, I was sorry to see him go. At the same time, I heard that Uncle Joe had been freed on bail and had promptly jumped it. The $20,000 that had found its way to someone in a position of power would have helped his bail application considerably. I was glad for him too, but couldn't help feeling jealous and slightly resentful. That's what happens when you are in prison.

Many a night I would sit cross-legged and stare up at the sky through the bars. There wasn't much else to do. Sometimes you could see the moon. This particular night it was like a clipped fingernail flicked onto a black velvet canvas. The guards opened the doors and called me over to them to save themselves trampling across the sleeping bodies. It was ten o' clock and I was immediately alarmed – in Thailand normal stuff didn't take place at night. I was handed over to two Thais in crisp dark suits who promptly handcuffed me and took me downstairs and outside to a waiting car where two more smartly dressed Thais were waiting. We sped away from the Immigration Centre and out onto the motorway, following the signs for the airport. As Thais often do, they assumed I could not speak or understand their language; I don't blame them, as precious few people who have English as a first language bother learning a second even when they live in another country, and the rest of the world is well aware of this. They were chattering excitedly about visiting Buckingham Palace, Tower Bridge and Madame Tussaud's; I could picture the plastic Union Jack-decorated bowler hats on their heads. I felt like telling them not to bother, the queues outside Madame Tussaud's would drive them mad, but more importantly it now became obvious that I was being accompanied to Heathrow Airport, where I would be handed over to New Scotland Yard. Now, I knew I was in a predicament here in Thailand, but I had not been charged with anything and was still confident that my money and sheer luck could get me out of trouble. Back in England I stood no chance and knew I was looking at a serious, serious lump of time or, worse still, onward transportation to America, where my life would be practically over. My blood ran cold.

At Bangkok's Don Muang Airport we passed middle-aged and elderly Englishmen exchanging anguished farewells with petite and pretty young Thai girls. The men's heads had been turned by being able to return their penises to active service when they'd thought all was lost, while the girls had their eyes firmly on the blue passport tucked inside their jackets.

My guards checked in their luggage and with no further ado we walked straight on to a scheduled Thai Airways flight, on which some seats had been reserved at the front of the plane. My mind was racing as I felt events overtaking me. Kindly, the guards soon removed my handcuffs and I twiddled my fingers and shook my hands to revive the life in them. I don't consciously remember deciding to do it but I then thumped one of the guards as hard as I could muster on the chin and the others started to shout and swear at me. They were shocked and certainly not expecting anything like that. I was shocked too: it was the first time in my adult life I had ever struck anyone. A steward minced towards me: 'What's happened sir?' I smashed him straight on the nose and blood spurted all down his uniform. He brushed some off with his finger, looked at it and then started screaming. By now the guards were on me, pulling me down on to the seats and trying to snap the handcuffs back on. The other passengers were shouting and screaming too, fearing, I suspect, a hijack or terrorist attack. They couldn't be sure who was the good guy and who was the bad guy here. Neither could I.

'They're kidnapping me,' I screamed. 'Someone call the police!'

Someone did call the captain.

'Take your seat,' he barked. Obviously no one had told him that a prisoner was being escorted on this plane. I managed to get an arm free and struck out, knocking his cap off.

'Get him off my plane,' he demanded.

'With pleasure,' I said and rushed down the gangplank with my Thai guards running behind me. They no longer had the excited, friendly faces they had been wearing on the way to the airport and I allowed them to re-handcuff me.

'You in big-time fucking trouble,' hissed one.

'Motherfucker,' spat another, obviously learning fast from his American friends.

After I was bundled back into the car we headed back into the city centre; the mood was dark. These guards were really upset and the guy sitting next to me was so seething about not getting to Madame Tussaud's that every now and then he just had to punch me in the face. He was so frustrated that he also started to pinch me like a kid.

I hadn't registered at first that instead of the guards sitting either side of me like on the way here, I was jammed up by the door with two of them practically sitting on me. The reason for this soon became clear when the driver shouted, *'Duen Nee'*, and swerved into the inside lane. This means 'now' or 'do it now'.

The man next to me threw himself across my body, lifted the

handle of the passenger door and shoved it open. He then threw himself back and, along with the other one, started to kick and push at the side of my body. I guess we were doing 60 miles per hour on the motorway, as the door was nearly blown off its hinges. Instinctively my fingers grabbed at whatever I could but it was difficult when cuffed. I didn't want to die. I could picture my brother reading the headline in his *Daily Telegraph* – DRUGS BARON DIES IN ESCAPE BID. Please God, don't let me die like this, I thought. I'm not that bad; like many people I tend to go all religious at extreme moments. Somehow I was clasping my would-be killer's leg just above the ankle and he was almost standing up in the back of the car trying to kick me out of it. God replied. I managed to slide down on to the floor between the front seat and the back seat still holding the ankle of one policeman. The other gouged at my eyes and both were kicking and kicking with their free legs. The man in the front passenger seat had climbed over to join in. Even the driver was shouting encouragement. This was the proper meaning of the word frenzy. Because of the confined space I was lodged in, there was little leverage for them to kick me out of the car. The pain from a thumb in my eye socket and the kicks, punches and ripping of my hair was immense, but the instinct to survive helped me not to focus on it.

After what seemed like an eternity the car slowed down and I can only guess that the driver had become concerned about the number of other cars in the next lane that were slowing down to watch, with some of them sounding their horns. Whether this was in protest at what they could see, or was the old traffic-accident blood-and-guts magazine mentality exciting them, I'll never know. It crossed my mind that the guards might now just pull over and put a bullet in my head but they merely allowed me to lie still, then leant across my trembling body and slammed the door shut. Then they helped me back into my seat, everyone resumed their seating arrangement and just looked ahead. Not another word was said as we headed back to the Immigration Centre. I swear they were embarrassed. It was bizarre: they had tried to kill me, I had tried to save my life. A burst of murderous activity all over in about one minute, though it had felt like ten. The entire surreal incident reminded me of a pervert schoolteacher making a clumsy sexual advance to one of his pupils, being vehemently rejected and then attempting to resume quickly the status quo.

Back at the Immigration Centre the guards could not disguise their delight at my return, even expressing concern over the cuts and bruises on my face. To them my first name was Meal, my second name, Ticket. After what had just happened, this place that had first felt like hell on earth seemed like home.

Before my attempted deportation I had instructed my Thai lawyer to serve a writ on the Thai Government for holding me illegally and, finally, some days after the bungled assassination attempt, it went to court. How elated I was after much courtroom argy-bargy when I deciphered that the judge was ordering my immediate release; but how dejected I was when a special plea from the DEA under RICO asked for my continued internment pending 'further investigation'. RICO stood for Racketeering Influential Corrupt Organisations. It was a wide-ranging US statute originally set up to aid the authorities in their war on the Mafia inside their own country but had now been extended to the likes of drug smugglers like myself. Under RICO there was no limit to the powers afforded to US agents and, like no other law, it was no respecter of foreign boundaries, governments and laws. Three further times I went back to the Thai court and three times I got the same result.

Back in the centre I made friends with a man called Tariq, who had been held there for an incredible two and a half years. He was Iranian but had been educated in England and was therefore fluent in English. James Ghana was a good mate but our conversations were limited by our poor understanding of each other's languages. Tariq had been a personal bodyguard and assistant to the Shah of Iran but fled his country when the Ayatollah forced the Shah into exile. He had ended up somehow in Thailand on a false passport and in here with us. He was not an economic migrant or a criminal and his situation was intolerable. The poor guy couldn't come to terms with it and there was no reason why he should. Representatives from the United Nations regularly visited him to discuss his case and their efforts to secure his release and arrange his resettlement in a friendly country of his choice. Neither he nor I could understand why this was taking so long. He did not have access to money, having had to up sticks at such short notice, but with the UN on his case we thought this shouldn't matter. His anxiety was tangible and of all the people in the centre he seemed the most ill at ease. He built himself up before each official visit only to plumb the depths of depression when the UN representatives broke the news of their lack of progress. His frustration and despair was alarming and I should have known (not that there was anything I could have done) that he was losing it when he began talking to himself and beating his chest with his fists. He said he would make the UN sit up and take notice. Over a period of weeks he collected cigarette lighters and emptied the fuel from them into a container. Two women and a man from the UN arrived one afternoon and talked to him through the bars.

'We are doing all we can,' said one of the women.

At that he flourished the container from beneath his white *thobe* and poured the contents all over himself.

'If I cannot be free, I will go to my God in flames. Make me a commitment,' he demanded as he pulled out a lighter and flicked the flame near himself. We all put it down to Middle Eastern dramatics and not for one minute did we believe he was doing more than making a scene. I'm sure that's what he actually intended because when he flicked the lighter he did so away from his body. It backfired, however, as the fumes ignited in a mini-explosion and his *thobe* just whooshed alight. It was horrific. It took a few seconds for anyone to act and not before the unforgettable stench of burning flesh had filled the room. He threw himself to the ground and the boys nearest him threw blankets on him and rolled him around the room as people scattered to escape the flames licking all over his body. A guard appeared at the bars, shouted something in Thai and then ran off to fetch the keys.

'Save him. Save him,' screamed one of the now hysterical UN women as the guard returned with reinforcements and unlocked the door. They wrapped him in more blankets and dragged him out of the cell. No attempt was made to see if he was alive or dead. If he wasn't dead, then he soon would be.

Time passed. Christmas came and went. My girlfriend supplied me with sleeping pills that knocked me out for 12 hours of the 24. Every now and then the place would almost empty as the Burmese and Vietnamese were gathered together and bussed back to their respective borders. Within a few hours, though, the place would be full to overflowing again as a load of new but similar faces arrived after being rounded up.

This place really was a business. You see, the Thai authorities were paid $5 per person per day by the United Nations to park these refugees. They say the key to success in the hotel industry is all about location, location, location. Here in the Thai Immigration Holding Centre it was all about occupancy, occupancy, occupancy.

My girlfriend resorted to the tried and tested method of getting things moving in Thailand and asked the Head of the Immigration Centre outright how much it would cost for me to be able to walk out of the place and just disappear. The reply was £100,000. She contacted one of my associates in England and gave him the number of a safety deposit box in an Amsterdam bank that contained almost £500,000 in sterling cash. This particular associate travelled to Holland and from there was to come to Thailand and deliver the cash to my girlfriend. After a week he still had not showed and I began to worry as my girlfriend could not contact him and the immigration people warned us that the particular window we were working on could close at any minute. Five fucking weeks later my associate arrived. He had the temerity to blame me.

'Philip, how could you have put me in such a predicament?'

'What the fuck are you on about?'

'I've never seen that sort of money before. It was ridiculous! I could have been locked up for money laundering.'

'Shut up. Have you sorted things?'

He looked sheepish.

'I've had a bit of a spend-up.'

I knew what was coming.

'I had some bets . . . bought a car . . . and a farm . . .'

And then he went into detail about where most of the money had gone. I was incensed, distraught and destroyed. I didn't give a fuck about him spending the money, but not bringing enough to get me out was unforgivable. It was too late by now anyway, as the immigration people had gone cold on the idea a couple of weeks earlier. I did forgive him in the end though. Well, he was my cousin.

I spent nine long months in the Immigration Centre. I have to confess that my incarceration did become more and more tolerable. My money had bought me space, comforts and hope of an end to the nightmare. The weeks were punctuated by regular visits to court and when the judge finally told my barrister that he ruled I was being held illegally and should be released immediately, I thought that was it. I had even got round to thinking it was all a big mistake, I'd put it down to experience, stay in Thailand and carry on where I had left off.

A week later the judge's ruling had not been adhered to. The barrister and I were back in court.

'Why has this man not been released?' demanded the judge, scanning the faces in court for an answer. No answer was forthcoming.

'Bring the Head of the Immigration Centre to me first thing in the morning,' he thundered, 'and tell him to bring Mr Hamrogue's release papers. If he fails to do so I will be issuing a warrant for his arrest.'

This was unheard of in Thailand – a judge threatening another senior Thai with arrest. No one goes against the system, but the judge obviously felt he was being personally undermined and I believe my barrister had cleverly worked on this.

The next morning we were all in court again, but there was no sign of the Head of the Immigration Centre. The judge issued the warrant for his arrest and personally signed some papers ordering my release that day. My barrister waved the paper at me. 'This is good. This is enough,' he said. I was taken back to the centre for signing out and the guards were all smiling and shaking my hand. We'd grown quite fond of one another. I handed out my possessions, such as they were, to my neighbours and said goodbye. The guards took me out into the office, still very jolly, and invited me to use the telephone. I phoned a boy to pick me up on his motorbike pronto. 'Before they change their minds,' I joked.

The Head of Immigration arrived before the boy. He had the look of a man of status who had just had a warrant for arrest served on him. He growled something at the guard who had just been signing me out then turned to me and said, 'We are going to detain you for 24 hours to make enquiries about your entry into Thailand.'

'You've had the past nine months to do that,' I replied in disbelief.

Suddenly the gates swung open to the courtyard outside and two black limos with four motorbike outriders swept in. Lights flashed and sirens wailed. The customary crowd had gathered outside the gates. The American Ambassador, whom I knew by sight and from the TV and newspapers, stepped out of the car and strode meaningfully to the office. Momentarily I thought – aye, aye, what's going on here? But he was looking straight at me. He was here because of me. He didn't speak to me though; exchanged some Thai with the Head and leaned forward and scrawled his signature. Then he was gone. The Head seemed to have softened a little and appeared genuine when he said, 'I am sorry, but the United States Government have formally requested your extradition.'

My boy arrived at this point on his motorbike. He could see I was crushed. 'They changed their minds,' I said.

My extradition order had come directly from the US Secretary of State. The Yanks had spent much time and money tracking us down and were cracking us up to be the largest drug-trafficking network in the world. They had started with Howard and radiated outwards. Howard Marks was portrayed as the mastermind and Mr Evil, but in fact there was no real network. There were much bigger fish than us, but none, I suspect, without organised crime connections and we were therefore easier and safer to target. We had felt naively secure because someone in the DEA was feeding us with information about who they were following, what hotels were being bugged and so on. In our arrogance we believed we were always one step ahead and had every angle covered. Personally, I believed I was untouchable because I was independent from Howard, kept a low profile and my activities lined the pockets of many people in Thailand. As I mentioned before, the Thais themselves did not see the export of Thai grass as very different from the export of any other homegrown commodity. They regarded me as a hard-working and ambitious captain of industry more than anything else. What I had underestimated was the extraordinary power of the Americans and the strength of the special relationship they enjoyed with Thailand. The Americans ploughed billions of dollars into Thailand in an effort to stem the flow of hashish and heroin into the United States. This was a revenue flow that the Thais relied on and, needless to say, as the cash cascaded down through the system, plenty of officials creamed off some for themselves. This formed the basis of the relationship between the United States of America and Thailand.

For some reason, the guards did not put me back into the holding cell but rather crudely handcuffed America's most wanted to the leg of the table in the office. That night, as I lay on the floor listening to the guard's television, I knew the game was up. A feeling of utter despair washed over me and I wanted to cry. It hit home that the Americans controlled my destiny, not the Thais, and ultimately I didn't have the sort of money that could influence them. It wasn't about money with the Yanks anyway. It was about defeating Phil Sparrowhawk, Howard Marks and other 'enemies' of the free world.

In the morning I was taken to Maha Chai, the Bangkok Central Prison, situated in the Chinatown district. When the guard from the Immigration Centre handed me over, I felt even more helpless. I knew of Maha Chai and had even visited friends inside before: it was an old crumbling institution built by the French about a century before and tales were rife of mules, hippies and chancers going in and never coming out. I had never considered myself a mule or a hippy and therefore the thought that I would end up somewhere like Maha Chai had never entered my head. In the reception area, a Thai man ambled over to me and mumbled something. I ignored him, as it is often best to do in these situations. He then tapped my glasses and said something else. The bastard wanted me to hand over my gold-rimmed spectacles. I'd only been in there five minutes. I told him to fuck off and fortunately he did.

I was left standing alone in my T-shirt and shorts in an open area and Thai prisoners wandered around me staring. Some approached me and spoke in Thai. I knew what they were saying – Where you from? What you in for? What your name? – but I didn't answer and pretended I couldn't speak any Thai. I thought it might come in handy later if everyone believed I couldn't speak the lingo. At least they would talk in front of me then and I might get some pointers as to what was going on. Eventually a very relaxed-looking guard came over to me and smiled reassuringly. 'Come with me.'

He led me into one of the two blocks that looked out onto the recreation area and walked me down a corridor with cell doors on either side. The cell he showed me into had a wooden floor and a barred window in the wall at the end. The walls were cream but were decorated with graffiti and stained with the blood of crushed mosquitoes and cockroaches. This was my new home. It didn't seem too bad. There were a few blankets rolled up, a water bottle, a cup and a few other bits and pieces. The personal space, compared to the Immigration Centre, was like rattling around alone in a country mansion.

The guard left me alone and wandered off, leaving the door ajar.

So far, so good. I walked back out into the yard and squatted down in the shade of the building, out of the burning sun. Suddenly I felt hunger pains. I had heard the expression before but this was the first time I had actually experienced them. I hadn't eaten or drunk anything since the day before yesterday, although that hadn't registered until now. The brain told the stomach and the stomach kicked out. I tried to put it to the back of my mind again. As the sun sank lower in the sky, the shadows cast by the two buildings grew longer and began to meet in the middle. There was no siren or command from any guards but all the prisoners began to wander slowly back towards their cells. I looked at my watch and noted it was ten minutes to six, then followed suit. At six o'clock the national anthem is played throughout Thailand and wherever you are, whoever you are, you are expected to stand to attention.

When I got back to my cell I was shocked to see 15 other prisoners in there. How naive of me to think, even for a few hours, that the cell was just for me. A Thai man who was a prisoner but what they'd call a trusty back at home led me by the arm to a small room adjacent to the cells and sat me down. He then got busy clamping irons around my legs just above the ankle and tethered them together with the heaviest chain imaginable. I tried to catch his eye so that, as he closed the irons on my legs, he'd leave some room but he would not make eye contact. The chain had enough slack to allow you to take small steps but you had to hold up the chain between your legs by some cloth tied around it to keep the irons from chafing your ankles. Job done, I shuffled back into my cell.

My fellow prisoners, most of whom seemed to be Thai, unlike those in the Immigration Centre, continued to bombard me with questions but I shook my head and repeated 'Am Irish' and feigned total incomprehension until they got fed up. As night fell, the guards looked in and took a quick headcount. I could hear them chattering and bantering with one another as they moved on to the next cell. Further up the corridor I could make out a television set and the compulsory whir of electric fans. There was little conversation in our cell and the men seemed to be content to pull the blankets over themselves and fall asleep. I did the same.

In the morning the doors were unbolted noisily at seven. I followed the men out into the yard in single file in what was obviously a well-rehearsed ritual. Only one other man from my cell was in leg irons. I wasn't sure if this was a good sign or not. We stood alongside a metal trough with a number of taps punctuating its length. The guard blew his whistle and we all stripped down and placed bowls below the taps, caught some water and threw it over our bodies. A second blow of the whistle signified refilling the bowl and this time we threw the water on to our heads. Third whistle and we grabbed some soap and started to rub furiously. Fourth whistle, more water to wash the soap away. Fifth and final whistle, get dressed and stand to attention. The boys from the next cell were waiting to take our place.

Whilst washing I made sure I sucked in as much water as I could. I had now not drunk or eaten for nearly three days. Ironically, when the food came at midday, I had trouble getting it all down. This prison obviously used the same contract caterers as the Immigration Centre. Shit, shit and more shit.

On the third day my girlfriend eventually found me again and she immediately sweetened the guards up with a few brown envelopes stuffed with cash. I was not allowed to see her but my leg-irons were whipped off. I found out later that they put these on you when you first arrive to stifle any thoughts you may be having about escaping, or if you have been a nuisance in any way. Bottles of water were handed over to me and a mattress was laid out on the floor. I had registered with the guards now and some even smiled and nodded at me. The other lads looked on in curiosity rather than jealousy but I could not explain anything to them. At least that's what they thought.

That night, more relaxed in the knowledge that my family knew where I was and with some small home comforts, I pondered my situation. My future was definitely in the hands of the Americans. What were they going to do with me? Allow me to rot in Thailand? Take me back to the States for a morale-boosting publicity trial and serve me up 30 years? Was there still a way of buying myself out? Then it dawned on me that I was only thinking of myself, and the image of my three-year-old daughter and my girlfriend kept thrusting itself to the front of my mind. My girlfriend, who had been dependent on me since she was a teenager, must have been worried sick and my little girl would be wondering where her daddy was. My thoughts drifted back to my childhood, to my own mum and dad, and my uncles and aunties, to my mates and to the quiet and quirky little Epsom town with its whitewashed grandstand standing majestically on the top of the Downs next to the winning post of the Derby racetrack. If they could see me now . . .

Part Two

THE BEGINNING

HORSES FOR COURSES – EPSOM, ENGLAND

Epsom lies on the edge of both Greater London and the rolling Downs of the Surrey countryside. On the main road out of the town there still stands a small stone that told horse-and-coach drivers of yesteryear that London is 14 miles away. And by London they meant St Paul's Cathedral or some other central landmark. The capital's close proximity and the abundance of railway lines passing through the town made it an ideal site for the housebuilders of the time to create commuter land in the 1920s and '30s. Epsom residents have the unusual luxury of three railway stations – Epsom, Epsom Downs and Tattenham Corner – all within a mile of each other (and numerous others within a five-mile radius) to take them on the half-hour journey to the main London terminuses. Gleesons, Burton, Harwood, Carter and Wimpey, the top housebuilders of the time, basically expanded Epsom and built up the surrounding countryside of neighbouring Ewell, Tadworth, Cheam and Stoneleigh to accommodate this new breed of middle-class inhabitant.

But Epsom had been around and played an important part in English life for centuries. Aristocrats had travelled to the town in large numbers since the sixteenth century to sample the famous, health-giving Epsom Salts and spas. Samuel Pepys records one such visit in his diary. King Charles is reputed to have used one of the many inns in the town for a bit of clandestine shagging of Nell Gwynn. But more notable is Epsom's fame as the premier horse-racing town in Britain and home of the Derby, the most famous horse race in the world. All these rich visitors and their entourages lolloping around Epsom, sniffing their salts in the seventeenth century would get a bit bored and so they began taking their servants and footmen up onto the rolling Downs overlooking the town and racing them against each other. Not a horse in sight. That is how it all started. Not a lot of people know that.

By the early 1600s horses had replaced servants. This idea possibly came from the weary footmen themselves. Within a hundred years the horse racing on Epsom Downs had become the premier sporting event of the year and a social occasion for rich and poor alike. The following poem was published in 1735 and not only conjures up the flavour of the occasion but if you strip out the archaic language it is still relevant today:

> *On Epsom Downs when racing does begin,*
> *Large companies from every part come in,*
> *Tag, rag and Bo-tail, Lords and Ladies meet,*
> *And, Squires without Estates, each other greet,*
> *A scoundrel here, pray take it on my word,*
> *Is a companion for the greatest Lord,*
> *Provided that his Purse abounds with Gold,*
> *If not, then his Affection will not hold.*
>
> *Here the promiscuous and ungovern'd Crew,*
> *Crowd to see what is neither strange or new,*
> *Bets upon bets, this Man says — Two to one,*
> *Another pointing cries, good Sir — 'tis done.*
> *See how they gallop o'er the spacious plain,*
> *As if pursu'd and dreading to be slain;*
> *Not half such speed would any of them make,*
> *To save their country if she lay at Stake.*
> *The races done, to Town the mob repair,*
> *Some curse their Fate, and some the Booty share.*

In 1779, The Oaks – the race for fillies – was first run and the following year saw the first-ever Derby Stakes, named after the Earl of Derby. These two races remain the highlights of the Epsom race meeting held in the first week in June. Come rain or shine, war or peace.

As the horse-racing industry grew, Epsom, naturally, and Newmarket in Suffolk, where the 1,000 and 2,000 Guineas were held, became home for all manner of owners, trainers and jockeys. Growing up I was very aware of the yards dotted around the racecourse run by men with wonderful names like Boggy Whelan, Staff Ingham and Scobie Breasley. I was even more aware of the boys and men who worked in the stables and frequented our pubs and betting shops in the afternoons and evenings. They stood out because they didn't stand out. In their game, if your body grew to a height of more than 5 ft 3 in, you were a giant. They had migrated to the town from all over the country and all shared the common dream of finding fame and fortune as a jockey. Ninety-nine out of a hundred would still be shovelling shit and riding out on the Downs at unearthly hours when they were in their 30s or 40s.

I was born in 1949 in Epsom District Hospital, then a modern building on the site of the former workhouse or spike, as it was known. In the workhouse days, homeless people were only allowed to stay for one night and were kicked out in the morning. Then they would walk all day the many miles to the next one. This is why they were called 'tramps' or 'gentlemen of the road'. The spike in Epsom was part of this sad route and for many years after the hospital was built, and even in my lifetime, the tramps would still pass through Epsom and doss down in the fields or derelict houses around where the workhouse had once stood.

Clothes and sweet rationing introduced during the Second World War was just ending as I was born. Down at the Odeon cinema in the town, the people of Epsom were filing through the gold-plated double doors to watch Orson Welles and Joseph Cotten in the film hit of the year, *The Third Man*. On the way out, as they queued for their bus or tucked into fish and chips from Marshall's next door, they couldn't help but hum the film's musical score – the haunting 'Harry Lime Theme'. If there had been a chart then, that song would have been number one.

In the dance halls, young people jitterbugged. The Americans and the Canadians had gone home but their dances remained. In the pubs, The Spread Eagle, The Albion, The Marquis of Granby, The Charter or The Eclipse, locals speculated on who would win the next month's Derby. A horse called Amour Drake was fancied locally but ended up finishing second to Nimbus. For those people in Epsom who could read, *1984* by George Orwell was doing good business in Pullinger's the bookshop.

Our home was on the Wells Estate, a small council estate that was plonked without thought in the middle of Epsom Common. The Common, unlike the rolling green Downs, was dense countryside teeming with wild birds and animals such as foxes, badgers and deer. There had been a country community on the Common for centuries living quietly, and up until not long before our arrival, off the land. To have an estate of semi-detached houses built in their midst must have been a massive shock. They lived in small red brick cottages around the Stamford Green pond or deeper into the Common in white-painted weather-boarded houses and were served by two pubs, The Cricketers and The Jolly Coopers, a working man's club, a church and a tiny shop or two. Older folk still spoke with a country burr of the kind that you find nowadays in deepest Devon or Dorset and were still accustomed to going out and getting dinner with a ferret or a gun. There are no old Common folk left now.

We were a happy family, me, my older brother, Tony, my sister, Audrey and our mum and dad. Or at least I thought we were.

My first school was just up the top of the road on White Horse Drive. It was a small infants' school, catering mainly for us kids from the Common, and stood shyly next door to the sprawling and renowned Rosebery Girls' School. Rosebery was a grammar school named after another toff, Lord Rosebery, who I understand was once an Epsom resident and a former prime minister. For many years his old Hansom cab was displayed in the little local museum. Even in my time the school advertised itself as a school 'for the daughters of gentlemen'. I never really understood what that meant. Who else could you be a daughter of?

There was no real expectation that I would pass the 11-plus exam, unlike my elder brother, and so at 11 years old I moved on to Lintons Lane school further down in Epsom town. It was here that my education really began. Lintons Lane was an academy for hooligans. This is where the ruffians went and pastimes were no longer blowing birds' eggs that we had taken from nests on the Common, or soaking conkers in vinegar, but smoking, shoplifting from Woolies and trying to get your hand up girls' skirts. I remember the headmaster had the unlikely Dickensian name of Mr Umpleby and my teacher was a weasely-looking man called Chick Chappel. Another master, Percy Roberts, doubled up as a local magistrate and thus continued to monitor many of his pupils' progress long after they had left school. We were expected to wear uniform (few did) and chant the school motto – some old bollocks about sincerity and endeavour.

I must admit I enjoyed the company of the rogues and felt at home there. I was one of them but never a ringleader or a scrapper like some. I was never a boy for confrontation with teachers, or other pupils come to that. Couldn't see the point. I did develop an interest in making money though. I'm not sure where it came from because I never recall thirsting for material possessions or being jealous of other boys. Perhaps there was nothing to get jealous about. It was probably genetic. My dad and his brother were businessmen with varying degrees of success, as I will explain. My grandfather had been a greengrocer in Hackney, east London, and his ancestors were all scrap-metal merchants and before that horse dealers. I don't think the Sparrowhawks had ever worked for other people.

There was a craze for Airfix models whilst I was at the school. The kids bought these kits in the shops and then spent hours in the evenings painstakingly constructing mainly warplanes and battleships with the aid of Airfix glue and a diagram. Finally they would paint them with Airfix paint and bring them to school, where they displayed them proudly to the other kids. The whole process could take a week of intense concentration; I can't see kids having the patience or the interest these days. Some kids in those days didn't have the patience or the interest either. I was one. But the boy who sat next to me loved it. He was brilliant; he never went out and could knock out the models faster and better than anyone I knew. His bedroom was full of Dakotas, Tiger Moths, HMS this and HMS that, all hanging from the ceiling and sitting proudly on shelves. I bet he's a precision engineer these days. I started buying the kits, handing them over to my new friend, and then taking them to school fully constructed and diligently painted and selling them on for double the price. The kid didn't even want any money. He saw it as some sort of challenge, locked in his bedroom hour after hour. He may have failed his O levels because of me.

Tony Ward was a good pal whom I met at school. He was a relaxed and laid-back boy with a keen interest in horse-racing. We used to tease him a bit but he took it all in good stead. His birthday was the 31st of March and we used to say he was born a day early. Mickey Dixon was also one of my best friends. He loved a bet, a fag and a pint, which may not have been totally normal for a 14 year old but it came naturally to him. He was also an easy-going, uncomplicated boy who continued to enjoy those simple pleasures for the rest of his life.

I'm sure it was partly because we grew up in a racing town, but Epsom was full of boys like Mickey, Tony and myself who read the *Sporting Life* in preference to *The Eagle*, *The Hotspur* or *The Dandy*. None of us junior punters seemed to win very often but when they did they liked to invest their winnings in packets of twenty cigarettes rather than the usual packets of five or singles they were normally forced to purchase.

Soon, I decided I would start to take the bets rather than place them. Half a crown here, three pence there. I even brought multiple copies of the *Sporting Life* into school to try and encourage the boys to gamble their pocket money and dinner money with me. When I paid out, I made a show of being grumpy but ensured as many of the other boys as possible saw me hand over the cash. It was an early lesson in psychology.

My father and my uncle Ernie were both bookmakers. At first they worked from home semi-illegally – or was it fully illegally? They took bets in pubs and clubs and offices. They made a living but, although my uncle seemed to be fairly prosperous, because of the then shady nature of the profession neither could really build their businesses. They then had one of those turns of luck that come along maybe once in a lifetime. They may be rare but they do come, though only a few of us notice them. Fewer still do anything about it.

In the early 1960s, the Government liberalised the gaming laws. It was no longer illegal to take bets. Street runners became a thing of the past and the first betting shops opened. Dad could now carry out his business openly and things improved for him, but Uncle Ernie leapt ahead, wasting no time in opening his first shop in Epsom. Now the punters came to him and he had them together in one place for entire afternoons. A captive market. This was heaven.

I spent more and more time with Ernie at his home or the shop. With Mum and Dad both working, I'd finish school and wander down to his shop next to The White Hart in Epsom town centre. I used to sit out the back with Ernie as he literally watched his tills fill up with notes. I was not allowed to wander into the shop area – Ernie was not going to risk this little goldmine being shut down by the authorities – but I could see in through the hanging plastic strips that separated the back office from the shop. There were no television screens in those days. Assistants scrawled out the odds on blackboards and races were broadcast over a tannoy. I'd watch as the men intensely studied the form from the *Sporting Life* pages attached to the wall with drawing pins. One would then exchange conversation with the man next to him, roll a cigarette and finally write out a bet and push the slip under the glass at the counter. If there were ten men intently listening to the progress of their horses, some shouting and urging them on, at the end of the race nine would screw their slip into a ball and either leave the shop or start studying the form of the next race. The other solitary one would hang around until the horses were weighed in and then collect his winnings. How fucking easy was that?

Sometimes a stable lad would come in and bet a large amount, or an unfamiliar face would arrive and pull a wad of notes from a posh leather wallet. This raised the spectre that someone had some inside information. Ernie then had to decide whether to lay off all or part of the bet with another bookmaker. This was his gamble and gave him his buzz. Laying off a bet was merely mirroring all or part of a punter's wager with another bookmaker as a hedge or form of insurance. Some days Ernie lost. But most days he didn't. Theoretically, if a bookie keeps a perfect mathematical book on every race he will never lose, but it is hard to do this continually, especially in the heat of the moment. It is hard also to resist the temptation to achieve a higher rate of return by not sticking to mathematical matching odds and not laying off large bets on outsiders. Nevertheless it was the perfect business model.

Dad eventually got a shop too and Mum went to work with him. They were not particularly happy together and I guess this is why I spent such a lot of time with Ernie. I didn't like being around acrimony. As I got older I learned that Mum had been 'carrying on', as they quaintly said in those days, for years with one of Dad's friends, and eventually she left Dad to go and live with this man. It broke his heart. I don't think it did me a lot of good either.

Perhaps knowing that I would find this out sooner or later, Ernie often imparted his wisdom about women to me. He didn't marry, although he enjoyed female company vigorously. 'They can't be trusted,' he would tell me. 'They are spenders not earners. You don't need them, Phil. Use them by all means, boy, but never let them use you. You never ever know what a woman is really thinking. They're not bad. They just do bad things. They can't help it. Keep them at arm's length – that's my advice.'

I would nod as he fed me all this wisdom but didn't really have the faintest idea what he was going on about.

Some boys stayed on at school and took exams. Well, I think there was one in my year. The rest of us stormed the school gates as soon as we were 15 to get out to work and earn money. My headmaster wrote on my leaving report that academically I was a failure, but I did show entrepreneurial abilities and he thought I could be a success in commerce, though there was a risk I could end up in prison. What extraordinary foresight. How thrilled my parents must have been with his comments.

Some of the boys would have gone on to work at one of the local hospitals. Epsom was home to a clutch of large Victorian mental asylums. Others would have gone straight to Ronson's, the lighter factory in nearby Leatherhead, or the Goblin household appliances factory in Ashtead. Their most famous new fangled product was the Goblin Teasmaid. Just the mention of it was enough to give us 15-year-old boys an erection. A few others would have become apprentice electricians, bricklayers and plumbers. Me, I knew where I was going. To Dad's betting shop in nearby New Malden, where else? My older brother Tony had shown much more academic ability and dedication than me, and had, to Mum and Dad's immense pride, gone on to university. I think Dad was also proud, though, to have me sitting out the back of the shop settling the bets. I was fast at it and got through more work than his normal paid employees.

I did this for a couple of years but soon became bored. I could settle the bets with my eyes closed. The punters were so regular in their habits I could have written their wagers for them too. I would have liked to have managed the shop but I was barely 17 and this would not have been possible legally or practically. I therefore applied for a job I had seen advertised in the *Epsom & Ewell Advertiser* at a large bookmaker called PTS in Leatherhead and was taken on. I'm not sure what Dad thought about that. PTS was basically a credit operation where punters held accounts and phoned in their bets. Their statements detailing winnings and losses were forwarded to them by post at the end of the week, month or quarter. About 40 girls manned the phones and took the bets, and it was our job, me and 25 other young hungry chaps, to approve the bets and make the book. We had to think fast, basically creating a book on each race and ensuring PTS couldn't lose. It was down to us to lay off where we judged it was necessary and we competed madly with one another to put in the best individual performance.

I can only compare what we did to trading on a stock exchange floor. I experienced a massive adrenalin rush as bets came in for hundreds of pounds. I personally took single bets that were larger than a full day's takings at Dad's shop. I had gone from painstakingly working out a two-shilling accumulator place bet on three favourites at Alexandra Park to considering £100 on the nose on a 10–1 shot. A guy called John Ward ran the show and he taught me a great deal in the two years I worked at PTS.

Mickey Dixon and Tony Ward from school joined me there and put their knowledge of horse-racing and love of gambling to good use. We, the settlers, maintained our own betting account and as we spotted trends in the market we'd place bets with other bookmakers and build up a pool, which we would share out every month. We gained enormous satisfaction from outwitting the public at one end and taking money from other bookmakers at the other.

Much of the 'inside' information gleaned about horses and specific races is nonsense. Racing towns such as Epsom or Newmarket thrive on all this gossip, especially in the pubs on Saturday lunchtime before the day's card is off. Most comes from the stable lads, who will happily tell you, maybe for the price of a pint or the loan of money to 'invest', that the horse they look after will win this afternoon. Of course, there is no way they can know this, but they do know if the horse is performing well in training and, more importantly, they may know if the horse and jockey will be trying or not. Everyone inside racing knows that in any race only some of the horses will seriously be trying to win or get placed, the others are there to make the numbers up, to justify the training fees to owners or merely to give the animal a run-out. Not everyone outside of racing realises this. In some cases a horse will be deliberately held so it does not win even though it could. This is in order to improve its odds (widen them) when it comes out next time so that potentially more money can then be made by the people in the know who are backing it. Therefore, knowing whether or not a horse will be trying is useful information indeed to the serious punter.

The reason that lowly stable lads are often in the know is precisely because they are so lowly. The lads were paid a pittance. Still are. It would not be possible to support a family, or pay for a mortgage, a council rent or even a record collection with the money earned as a stable lad. They live in digs, often with other lads sharing the same room, and are probably one of the last examples of a seriously exploited workforce in this country. They're not that much better off than the footmen that were raced against each other on Epsom Downs 300 years ago. They still doff their caps to the trainer and address him as 'Sir' or 'Guv'nor'. For the entertainment of the owners and other worthies they are often expected to box each other too.

The trainers and the industry take advantage of the lads' youthful ambitions in the first instance and, as they grow older, their limited options. It's a scandal and one way the trainers ease their guilt over the paltry amounts paid to these boys and men is by tipping them off when their horses are going to be trying and they believe they have a good chance of winning. The lads will then invest part of their earnings on said horse, plus pass the information on to a web of contacts, who, if successful, will bung them a few quid for the tip. The trainers must love it – paying a bonus to their employees with the employees' money. The irony, however, is that these webs of contacts are rarely closed and, as the information spreads and the bets fly on and the price offered by the bookmakers comes down, sometimes the trainer and owner may make the decision to make the horse not try and wait for another day and a better price.

At PTS we got to know who the real punters were. Some were trainers, some were owners and some were professional gamblers. We'd get to see the bigger picture. We'd get to know who seemed to have good information. If a chap was continually backing rank outsiders who were winning, we'd know he had information. We'd know to lay him off. We'd know to follow him with a small punt of our own. But if a trainer had also had a large uncharacteristic bet in the same race on his own competing horse, we'd know to be cautious. We knew that the trainer was trying too and he believed that his horse could win, so much so that he was backing it with his own money. We might only lay off half the big punter's bet. It was an exciting time and I started to become addicted to the adrenalin rush of gambling. PTS taught me that gambling is fun and if the odds are in your favour – and there are ways of ensuring they are – it can also be lucrative.

But I was never going to get rich working for PTS or anyone else, so I began to form plans in my mind to branch out on my own and build up some serious capital. Although I was only 18 and had been out at work only three years, I felt that I had served my apprenticeship. I went to work for Uncle Ernie at his shop for £16 a week but we had an understanding that I'd do a bit off my own back. I built up a clientele of shopkeepers, publicans, businessmen and drinkers who'd place their wagers with me when I popped in to see them all as I walked through Epsom town on a Saturday morning. I'd give them better prices (I had no overheads); I came to them and enjoyed a rapport with them as customers. I suppose I was a door-to-door bookmaker on a Saturday.

It was the late 1960s. Some of my contemporaries had turned into hippies, wearing their hair long and sporting beads and the yellow teeth of animals strung around their necks. I'd see them standing in the Harlequin record shop flicking through the album covers. 'Hello, man,' they'd say.

I couldn't work them out. I was busy earning. I had £100 in my back pocket from punters. No time to salivate over the psychedelic cover on the latest Incredible String Band album for me. Conversely, other boys from school and around the area had started cropping their hair in the style of American soldiers and wearing a uniform of Ben Sherman shirts, Levi jeans, braces and leather Dr. Marten boots halfway up their legs. Sid the Yid on the market was coining it in selling them all the gear. They were in the record shops too, but they didn't waste any time, just grabbed the latest *Motown Chartbusters* LP, tucked it under their arm and then took off home to play it on their tinny old gramophone. If anything, as the two youth cults polarised, I leant towards the latter. I suppose I had been a Mod, the skinhead's older brother, but I hadn't really noticed or become excited about any of these youth explosions. I had no time for Bank Holiday jaunts down to the seaside to engage Rockers or fight other gangs of youths in the local dance halls. Strangely, looking back on it I never really saw myself as a youth at all.

Tony, my brother, had embraced the hippy lifestyle with enthusiasm down in Brighton, where he was attending university. Now and then I would travel down to see him but must admit I didn't really feel very at home with his new circle of friends. I found it hard to take seriously people wearing bells around their necks who spent their days lying horizontally on mattresses and blowing pungent smoke rings into the air. He did introduce me to one interesting guy though.

Nicky had made a million by the age of 16, or at least that's what he told me. Driving around in a Rolls Royce and touring numerous properties in the Brighton area that he already owned, I saw no reason to disbelieve him. As a kid he had hit on a brilliant idea and it was from that that the first fortune came.

Kids from mine and Nicky's generation still had weird things called hobbies. Remember them? I mentioned Airfix models earlier, trainspotting was another, as were bird-watching and bird-nesting, but one that was particularly widespread in the 1950s and '60s was stamp collecting. Kids, particularly boys, would collect stamps ravenously and build up treasured albums as well as trading them at school and more widely with other collectors. I doubt if anyone under the age of 70 partakes these days. Not so many stamps around for a start. You don't need a stamp for e-mail, do you? Nicky started to buy stamps wholesale and packaged a lucky-dip variety into small clear plastic wallets that he then sold to newsagents to sell to the young collectors. His master stroke was to purchase from Stanley Gibbons, the stamp auctioneers, a small selection of rare and valuable stamps that were slipped into one bag in every thousand or so. It was the 1960s equivalent of the £50-note-in-the-crisp-packet offer. Nicky made a killing. I can remember buying the stamp packets myself, but lost interest quickly when my purchases yielded no Penny Blacks.

I don't know if Nicky thought I looked rough or something, but one day in 1969 he asked me if I knew anyone who could remove some squatters from one of his properties on Vere Road in Brighton. There was £100 in it for whoever could do it. I rounded up a couple of mates: one was Tony Ward from school, and the other was Roy Dean. Roy was a few years younger than us but he was bigger, had all the best skinhead gear and looked the part. Tony and I were not particularly handy with our fists and Roy was still a boy, but we figured that removing peace-loving stoned hippies should be easy. Hopefully they'd be comatose on their mattresses. Couldn't understand why Nicky didn't do it himself.

When we arrived, I asked Nicky what exactly he wanted us to do. He said he would like us to kick the door in and also put a ladder up to the roof and punch a hole in it.

'Make a hole in the roof?' I queried.

'Exactly. Even these scum will not want to be living in a house with no roof.'

We got to work. Tony and I got on the roof and started ripping the tiles off and hurling them down into the garden. Roy was shouting and threatening the hippies in their hallway. Nicky was nowhere to be seen. There was such a commotion that soon all the neighbours were out in the street and the police turned up. They called for us to come down but we pretended we couldn't hear. From somewhere a photographer appeared and Tony and I were snapped coming backwards down the ladder. In the confusion we managed to get away without any serious intervention from the Sussex

Constabulary. In the following Sunday's *News of the World* there was an exposé of the 'boy landlord' and his questionable methods of dealing with tenants. That was the first and only time I was described as someone's henchman.

By now, back in Epsom, I was making between £100 and £150 a week on top of my wages from Uncle Ernie's shop. This was a fantastic amount of money. I had calculated that within two years I could buy a nice house in Epsom – for cash. I was living well but still managed to put a ton a week away and delighted in watching my capital grow. My ambitions for what I would do when I had my first small fortune were boundless. The only difference between me and the rich people was money. Simple. Nothing else. And despite what everyone tells you and the way you are conditioned to think from the day you are born – it is out there to get. Money doesn't belong to anyone. Nobody has a divine right to it. The people who currently have it just don't want us getting our mucky paws on it. Who can blame them? We'd be the same if we had it. Uncle Ernie was becoming seriously rich now. He was clearing £1,500 a week and was driving a new top-of-the-range Jaguar. He'd even got himself a bird. Perhaps he was softening?

I went on like this for a couple of years until the summer of 1970, by which time I had £4,000 saved up in the Martin's Bank. I was on course – for what I wasn't sure. I remember the time so well. The England football squad had returned from Mexico, empty-handed but not disgraced. Their silly 'Back Home' record had been top of the charts. The Beatles announced they had split up officially but everyone had known it was coming. A song about Abraham Lincoln, Martin Luther King and John F. Kennedy sung plaintively by Marvin Gaye hung in the air. A general election was in the offing. Harold Wilson was expected to win but Ted Heath would eventually triumph. But most importantly, for me at least, a horse called Nijinsky had ridden into view.

There had not been another horse like him before and there has not been one since. Everything about him was right. He looked great. Even the way he read on paper was aesthetically pleasing, with the three dotted letters together. Other horses were not in the same league. Lester Piggott was the jockey for the Derby and I just knew they would win. I couldn't believe my luck when I could get, briefly, 9–4 odds weeks before the big race. I did agonise a bit, but not for long. One side of me told me to stake only half of my money. The other side said, have the courage of your convictions, man, there's plenty more where that came from. I soon knew it was my destiny to stake my entire savings and I did just that. I imagine it was one of the larger single bets staked that year and I had to spread it across a number of bookmakers.

I felt no nerves on that first Wednesday in June 1970. It was a lovely day and, as I walked into town, Epsom was almost at a vehicle standstill as the open-topped buses packed with already pissed raucous men and women snaked their way up Ashley Road to the course. Epsom railway station disgorged punters by the hundred every few minutes and the old green buses waited to take them up to the course. Rolls Royces, Daimlers and Bentleys gleamed in the sun and attractive ladies sat inside in wide-brimmed brightly coloured hats, exchanging banter with local youths through their open windows. I nipped up some back roads, avoiding the worst of the crowds, and was soon weaving my way through the parked cars to the grandstand.

I had rarely missed a Derby; it is such a momentous event for Epsom people. As kids we all had the afternoon off school legitimately. There were lots of opportunities for scamming a few quid: from donning white coats and pretending to be car-parking attendants, to sneaking behind the beer tents and lifting beers from the crates. You didn't even have to scam; it was common for happy and inebriated punters to bung the kids a coin or two and drunks often dropped their crumpled banknotes as they pushed them back into their pockets after collecting a bet or paying for a round. We'd spend the money in the funfair across the road. From the top of the Big Wheel you could see right across south London. There were birds galore and you'd watch them on a ride called The Rotor, where gravity held them against the wall as the floor disappeared and their skirts and dresses blew up over their faces. You'd pray for one not wearing knickers – there never was. One of the Epsom boys got a job riding his motorbike on the Wall of Death and we used to go and see if he'd fall off and hurt himself. I think one day he did.

In those days, back over on the course, you could squeeze up right next to the winning post. If you craned your neck you'd see the horses come around Tattenham Corner bunched together in an indeterminate multi-coloured blob. As they approached, the noise from the crowd increased as if someone was turning a volume knob. It would come down in waves from the hill and then you'd hear the thundering of the hooves and suddenly they were on you. The snorting of the horses, the crack of the whip and the cacophony of the crowd shouting the name of their horse or jockey, or more likely 'Go on my son.' For a couple of seconds you were virtually cheek-to-cheek with the jockeys and could almost feel the swish of the brightly coloured silks while watching Lester's determined frown with deep lines furrowing his cheeks as if they had been carved into stone; or Willie Carson, tufts of hair sticking out from under his cap with a grin as wide as the course lighting up his face.

If you had won, you'd scurry off to the on-course bookmaker to collect your few quid. As a boy you'd worry he might have folded up his pitch and scarpered to avoid paying you your 1/9d. When you got there, 30 others would be in front of you. If you were lucky enough to get handed a couple of green pound notes you'd fold them and put them in your back pocket casually, but hoping someone that knew you had seen. If you were old enough, you'd stroll over to The Rubbing House, get yourself a lager and sit around with the day-trippers from London, the gypsies and the drunks and discuss the merits of the runners in the next race. Derby Day is one of the few events where English people, rich and poor, old and young, black and white, have relaxed conversations with people they have never seen before and will never see again.

Nijinksy led almost from the off, with Lester piloting him perfectly. As they came around Tattenham Corner, he opened up a lead of a couple of lengths and I knew he had it. He won by two and a half lengths from a horse called Gyr but there was no contest. The starting price had been 11–8 but because I got in early I had done better than that. I cheered Nijinsky home but don't remember going mad, just feeling some relief. I had won over £8,000 and my small fortune was now swollen to over £12,000. To put this in perspective, it would be worth between £200,000 and £300,000 in today's money. I bumped into my pals Roy Dean and Mickey Dixon and a few of the other Epsom lads and although I told them I had had a good win I didn't tell them how much. We headed up to London and I took them all to The Penthouse Club, where I went on the blackjack tables and nicked another grand. When your luck is in, your luck is in. You have to ride it.

Dad was not so lucky at this time. Not only had Mum left him and moved up north to marry the man he had thought was his friend, she was also chewing his bollocks off financially. Dad was struggling money-wise and his confidence and zest for life had been shattered. I was able to loan him £6,000 of my newly acquired dosh to pay off his mortgage and ease his money problems.

I was still with Ernie but was now actively looking around for a new challenge. I could always take and make bets but now I wanted something more solid, something I could build up. I wanted to use my capital to launch a 'proper' business. I wanted an office, a car, a product. There was something about horse racing that people didn't regard as legitimate, not that that really bothered me. I didn't care what people thought but I did want to make my fortune off my own back. I wanted to be different from Dad and Uncle Ernie.

STREET LIFE
– LONDON, ENGLAND

By now I was going out with a local girl called Sue. She was very local, living across the road from our house on the Wells estate. Our families knew each other and we had walked down to the Saturday-morning pictures together among a group of other kids when we were very young, but had never really taken much notice of each other. There was no explosive love affair, we just sort of drifted together and found we got on really well. We became boyfriend and girlfriend and after six months decided to get on to the property ladder.

This was long before Mrs Thatcher started encouraging council tenants to buy their council houses. It was 1971, but people around Epsom generally seemed to be aspiring to own their own houses. Put your money in bricks and mortar, I was often told. This made more sense than handing it over a bar or a bookmaker's counter. House values were starting to rise and for me it was a no-brainer. Why pay rent and end up with nothing at the end? People who agonised over such things baffled me. I could not fathom people who continued to pay rent to councils or private landlords when they could afford to pay a mortgage. In the circles I moved in there seemed to be a lingering belief that people like us *shouldn't* own the roof over our heads. Bollocks to that. To pay a mortgage when you had cash was pretty fucking stupid too. If you borrowed £10,000 you'd end up giving the building society three times that over thirty years.

Nonsensical. We purchased a nice property in a small village called Walton-on-the-Hill, just the other side of Epsom Downs, for £12,000. I put £6,000 in from the Nijinsky cash and borrowed the other £6,000 from the building society. I intended to repay that at the first possible opportunity.

Meanwhile, on my occasional visits to London, I had noticed the street traders on Oxford Street and I started to pay careful attention to them. I saw them set up stall with a couple of fruit crates and then open a suitcase full of cheap jewellery. One would then whip up a crowd and knock the entire contents out to hungry shoppers, sometimes in minutes. The gear wasn't nicked; I could see that no self-respecting thief would bother to lift this stuff, but it was just cheap. Not quite end-of-the-pier material, but a million miles from Asprey and Garrard. There were very few down-market jewellers on the high street at that time: Ratner's had yet to come along and fill the crap gap, and this 'tom', as the traders called it (rhyming slang with tomfoolery/jewellery), was even hallmarked. So the stuff was saleable, but more than that the traders were using psychology again. The very nature of the way they set up, constantly looking around for the police, made the public curious, and when someone bought, they all clamoured to do so, terrified they would miss these incredible bargains. Any minute now the trader would have to snap his briefcase shut and scoot off. It seemed so easy – it was.

It occurred to me that although you saw these traders on the busy Oxford and Regent Streets in London you never ever saw them in the provinces. Maybe the crowds would not be big enough for them or the police, with less to do, would be more vigilant. I decided I'd give it a try, reasoning I had little to lose. My stock would be legitimate. Street trading was illegal but in the scheme of things it was taken as seriously as parking on yellow lines. More often than not these people were simply moved on. I chose to set up in Portsmouth on a Saturday; it seemed busy and no one knew me there. I hurriedly set up outside Woolworths and fought to overcome my basic shyness as I laid my necklaces, rings and charm bracelets out on a little trestle table.

'Come on ladies and gents. We haven't got a lot of time. Don't ask no questions and you'll get told no lies. Where else can you get a lovely gold bracelet like this – hallmarked and all – one pound? No joke. One pound. Go on, take it. I've got 25 of these. When they've gone, they've gone. Quiet, please. Quickly now.' Del Boy eat your heart out.

The first time I felt a bit of pratt, especially as I was addressing one solitary expressionless old lady with crumbs of doughnut around her mouth, but sure enough a crowd soon formed and by midday I had sold every single item in my case. I had spent £60 with the wholesaler the previous day and now had £250 in my back pocket: a fair old margin and all in three or four hours. I was delighted. Next time I spent £120 with the wholesaler, and so on. Soon I was taking lads from Epsom with me to act as lookouts and then a couple of the lookouts picked up the spiel and started trading themselves. I paid them £10 or £12 for what was normally a morning's work and a bit of commission if they were selling. The boys in Epsom, where the average weekly wage was still only £20 or so, were queuing up to do a Saturday with me.

One pal who came with me often was Dennis. One particular week things were going badly and I didn't think I'd even have enough to pay Dennis at the end of it. I bought a trade paper and noticed an advertisement for factory-damaged knickers up in Nottingham. I had a feeling about it and Dennis and I headed straight up the M1 to take a look. When we got there, the 'slight damage' referred to in the advert was actually that the knickers had three leg holes and no hole for the waist. Having said that, they were made from quality Nottingham lace. There were 8,000 pairs and they wanted only £1,000 for the job lot. This was a grand more than I had on me, though, and frankly I thought that even we would be challenged to sell these. Three-legged women were rare then, even in London. I was about to walk away but Dennis held a pair against himself, stretching one leg hole to show that it could take a waist – a slim one anyway.

'I'm not sure my boss will want these. Can I ring him please?' The factory manager allowed me into his office and I had a pretend conversation with the dialing tone.

'He says to bring him down a sample and if he likes them he'll take the lot.' The factory manager agreed to this and for some reason allowed us to take 1,000 pairs of knickers as a sample. The next morning we set up on a couple of boxes on Victoria Station and while Dennis held up a pair, stretching the third leg with his thumbs, I gave out the patter. We went out at 99 pence and did the lot over the course of the day. The following morning we returned to the factory, handed over the £1,000 we had taken and loaded up the remaining 7,000. In a couple of weeks we had moved the whole lot. I even contemplated calling the Nottingham factory and asking them to specifically make more three-legged undies to order.

In 1972, Sue and I got married. We nearly didn't. Unfortunately our wedding day coincided with Oaks Day at Epsom and my brother and I were running a book up on the track. At half past two in the afternoon he was becoming agitated. He was my best man and had certain responsibilities.

'Come on, Phil, they'll be getting worried.'

'Let's wait and watch the big race,' I said.

'We can't. The Oaks is at 3.15 and you get married at 3 p.m.'

Reluctantly I handed over the book to one of my assistants and got in the car, changing into my wedding suit en route from the Downs to the Christchurch Church on Epsom Common. Only at West Hill did we overtake the wedding car and saw Sue watching me struggle into my trousers. She was not amused. The vicar did his bits and pieces and then we were all out on the lawn outside Christchurch for the photos. I was not able to hang around and annoyed Sue by rushing off. I told Sue that I had to go back up and collect the money from the book on the Downs and would meet her at the reception at the Chalk Lane Hotel. We got very pissed back up on the course and upset both families by arriving back at the reception clearly the worse for wear. It was not an auspicious start to married life and I remember we had a really bad row.

Things soon settled down, though, and Sue knew what I did but didn't really take much interest. As long as the bills were paid and I was bringing money in she seemed to be happy. She never raised the subject of having children and never gave me a hard time about my unconventional hours and lifestyle. If I were Uncle Ernie, I would have been suspicious.

When I was street trading one day, a guy remarked casually that I should go to Blackpool in the holiday season. He said it was packed with holidaymakers, all with money in their pockets and feeling happy and relaxed. I didn't even know where Blackpool was – there was no racecourse there – but I could see the logic in what he was telling me. One of the lookouts and I went up on the train lugging a big brown suitcase each, both of which were full to the brim with cheap watches, a range of jewellery and other trinkets. I had spent a full £1,000 with my man in Berwick Street who was now supplying me, and the more I bought the better prices he was giving.

Blackpool is further than it makes out it is and the journey took several hours. We booked into a bed and breakfast and then the following morning set out along the Golden Mile until we found a closed-up snooker hall in the middle of the main shopping area. I had a slightly better flash now (flash being the market trader's window display), with fold-out boards covered in black velvet to display the goods on, and we set up. As soon as I opened my mouth, the crowds gathered. They were mainly northerners but there were plenty of Scots in town too. I think they heard me and thought . . . Cockney . . . flash . . . wideboy . . . bargain? I had never seen anything like it: they were jostling each other and waving their banknotes at us to take. People saw the crowd and literally ran across the street to see what was happening, and before they had even looked at the goods had whipped their wallets and purses out. This was my psychology theory being demonstrated in the extreme. I was worried though, because the crowd had spilled off the pavement into the road and angry motorists were sounding their horns in unison. Through the crowd, above the bobbing heads, my lookout saw a distinctive pointed black helmet and we packed our cases up and legged it. Back at the bed and breakfast house we couldn't believe that we had sold over half our entire stock in just less than two hours. We emptied our pockets and counted up just over £2,000!

The following morning we went back to the same spot, fairly confident that if we could get a police-free run at it we'd have offloaded all our stock and turned one grand into four, and we'd only been away from home three days. We hadn't really got started, however, when the police turned up. The lookout had been too busy taking dough to see them and we were arrested and bundled into a little light-blue panda car. The punters who had purchased were even more delighted now, utterly convinced that they had acquired illicit goods at knock-down prices. Our goods were taken from us and the money on our persons, which amounted to £800, was also confiscated. We were charged and put in the cells overnight to appear in the magistrates' court the following morning. My lookout pal was more than a little worried.

'Don't worry, you don't go to prison for street trading,' I reassured him.

'But why are they keeping us in the cells? Why haven't we got bail?'

'Because we're bound to hang around if they bail us, aren't we?'

In the morning we stood next to each other in the dock. We'd followed a drunk and disorderly, an elderly prostitute and a vagrant. The magistrate reminded us we were before him for trading on the street without a licence.

'I have no option but to fine you £5. We do not want to see you again. Do you understand?'

'Yes, your honour.'

He made no other comment and, to my amazement, as we left the court the police handed back our bags full of gear and the £800.

My lookout boy wasn't too happy when I headed straight back to the snooker club and started setting up again.

'How bad is that, £5? I'm happy to pay that every day,' I told him.

Before long the two coppers were back, the same ones that had nicked us the previous day.

'What the blazes do you think you're playing at?' the older one demanded.

'I'm trying to feed my wife and kids,' I offered, somewhat disingenuously.

'Are you planning on working up here all the time?' he asked, his tone softening a little.

When I nodded, he took me by the arm and guided me into an alley that ran down the side of the snooker club. I had no fear that he was going to beat me up. This was 1972, Dixon still ruled Dock Green, even if he was 87 and had a gammy leg.

'If you want to work here, it will cost you £100 a week and you drop it into the boxing club round the corner there, all right?'

'Done,' I smiled and proffered my hand, but he turned and walked away. This was my first experience of police corruption and I have to admit I was a bit disappointed. The money was not a problem — £100 a week was a drop in the ocean compared to what we were taking — but I didn't like to think that our dear non-armed police force was corrupt. I had heard stories about policemen letting speeding motorists go after having a crisp £5 note pressed into their hands and the old joke about offering a donation to the 'police ball' but this was pretty barefaced.

I stayed in Blackpool for the entire holiday season and returned home only to replenish my stock. The police did not bother me again, as I paid up my £100 as regular as clockwork. The takings didn't match the heights of that first day as people became accustomed to seeing me and therefore less convinced about how 'hot' the goods really were, but we had trading bumps every week when new holidaymakers pitched up and we did very well. I did the following season in 1973 too.

I bought a little van and fell into a routine – worked the week in Blackpool and came home each weekend and relaxed. Everything was fine. So I thought. I even fell into the habit of treating myself to little holidays. Weeks in the Seychelles or weekend breaks in Spain. I worked hard and felt I deserved it but I should have asked Sue if she would have liked to come with me. I was never a jealous or possessive person and when she said she wanted to go to Australia for a holiday with the girls, I was quite happy about it. It made me feel less guilty about my solo sojourns in the sun. After she returned, however, one late-autumn Friday night in 1973 I pulled up outside the house after the long and tiring journey from Blackpool and noticed an estate agent's For Sale board in the garden. When I looked closer, there was a strip saying SOLD stuck diagonally across it. Must be meant for next door, I thought. When I went inside, though, there was no one in. Also there was nothing in. Every solitary piece of furniture had gone, including the ornaments. I drove around to Sue's mother's house.

'Where's Sue?'

'She's moved, Phil. She needed space,' she replied sympathetically. When a woman says she wants space, that means she wants to leave you, she's shagging someone else or she wants to shag someone else. Nothing else.

'She's moved. Just like that. Sold our house behind my back. Where to?'

'Australia.'

'Aus-fucking-tralia?'

'Yes, she's gone to start a new life. You weren't exactly a good husband, were you Phil? Sue must have the only wedding photographs where the groom is looking at his watch.'

She had a point and I couldn't get angry with Sue's mum. Her parents were decent people and I had always got along with them. She explained that when Sue visited Australia she had liked it so much she decided she wanted to live there. I smelt another man. I went around the corner and told my dad. He'd been there before.

'Have a cup of tea,' he said as he plonked the kettle on the hob and lit the gas.

I had stupidly put the house in Sue's name. I had thought it was safest and tax efficient. By tax efficient I meant that I didn't pay tax, therefore a nice house, fully paid up by now, in my name could have invited unwelcome scrutiny. Big mistake. I understand she got nearly £30,000 for it. Sue had also emptied our bank account. Another ten grand to bolster the Aussie economy. At Dad's, as we drank our tea, I realised that the only assets in the world I possessed were the little van outside and the couple of hundred pounds in my pocket. Easy come. Easy go.

A few months later I received an official letter from Australia informing me that my wife had filed for divorce and the case was to be heard in a Melbourne court. The tone of the letter implied that I was being told for information purposes only and that pissed me off. So I jumped on a plane for the two-day flight to Australia. On the day, I slipped into the court and could see Sue sitting a few rows in front of me with a man. They were holding hands. That was something we had never done. The judge mumbled on for a few minutes then looked up at the handful of people dotted around the courtroom and said something in legalese which I interpreted as – does anyone present have any objections?

'No objections, your honour,' I said loudly from the back of the court.

Sue swung around and nigh on fainted as she saw me sitting there, arms folded, as bright as a button.

On the steps of the court she came over and spoke whilst her boyfriend hung around behind. 'I'm so sorry Phil. You do understand, don't you?'

I gave her a kiss and said that I did. It was true, I did understand. Uncle Ernie had told me what women were like all those years before.

THE KIMONO KID
– LONDON, ENGLAND

My brother Tony had graduated and become a pharmacist. He had a good job in Brighton but had been in a bad motorbike accident and nearly lost his leg. The leg continued to give him pain and whether it was because of that I don't know, but somewhere along the line he started taking heroin. By 1974 he was addicted to smack. Heroin had not infiltrated the mainstream by then. I certainly never came across it on the streets of Epsom or in the circles I mixed in. There was cannabis aplenty and purple hearts, black bombers, speed and even LSD. We only heard about heroin in connection with the deaths of rock stars but I guess Tony was moving in different circles.

Dad had remarried and was happier. Things were easier with Mum and I visited her when I could. My sister was living with her boyfriend and Ernie had retired to spend more time with his money. I was building up my capital again through street trading but the novelty was wearing off. Competition from the market stalls was increasing and even the shops were selling cheaper and cheaper jewellery. I moved into Capo di Monte 'porcelain' figures. They went wild for a while but of course they were fake. I bought them from a warehouse on the Commercial Road but the public loved them as long as I could convince them they were stolen. By now I had developed an impressive range of furtive and hunted expressions to accompany my sales patter but there was no hiding the fact I was turning into your ordinary run-of-the-mill market trader and that was not how I had envisaged myself. Again, I was looking for a way out. A friend came to me with an idea for a glazing shop on Ruxley Lane in Ewell and I gave him £5,000 to get it off the ground. He went out and bought a top-of-the-range motorbike. The shop lasted three weeks. Another £5,000 down the drain. Another friendship ruined by money.

Meanwhile, Tony got two years inside for importing hashish. None of the family could believe it. He was the brainy one who went to university. He had the good job. He was putting the Sparrowhawks on the map of respectability and now he was doing bird. I knew about his habit but I had put this down to his accident and the fall-out from the student lifestyle; it would pass, hopefully. I never viewed him as a person who would get himself into trouble with the law. A 'friend' of his from university had called him from Pakistan to ask if he could post some blow to Tony, suggesting that they could use some for themselves and then split the profits from selling the remainder. Tony agreed but thought it best for the puff to be sent to a post office box address rather than his own. When he went to collect the package, surprise, surprise, the Old Bill were there to meet him.

When I went to see him in prison, he was in a real state. They'd weaned him off heroin and he was now dependent on methadone, the heroin substitute. By the time he got out he was addicted to paracetamol.

'What on earth made you do that for fifty fucking quid?' I asked him.

'Fifty quid? Who said anything about fifty quid?'

'That's all you'd get for a bit of blow.'

'Fuck off, that blow had a street value of at least a grand. That's why I'm in here.'

That was the first time I can recall thinking about the possibilities of trading hashish.

I didn't think it about it for long, however, because along bowled my old Epsom mate Roy Dean. You know a Roy. Everyone knows a Roy. We went to school together, although he was a couple of years below me, and knocked around the pubs of Epsom a bit. He was tall, well built and blond with deep, sparkling blue eyes. He was a good-looking boy and man and, unfortunately for them, the girls could not resist him. His good looks made him confident and Roy could charm the birds from the trees. Men and women alike found themselves captivated by him; unless they knew him of course. Roy was an early medallion man and endowed with a very hairy chest, which he got out at the first opportunity. It could be at freezing point outside but Roy would be standing around with his shirt undone to his belly button, possibly in shorts. He could bullshit for England and really should have gone into double-glazing or selling cars but that was not for Roy. Life was one big adventure and he liked not knowing what was going to happen to him next. I had the entrepreneurial and organisational skills he lacked and he had the interpersonal skills and natural charisma that I had to work so hard at. Perhaps we saw this in each other.

'Philip, old son, get into silk kimonos,' he said earnestly. He often called me 'son' even though I was older than he was. I don't know if Roy had just shagged a lady who wore a silk kimono but something had convinced him they were the next big thing.

'You get hold of them and I will be able to sell as many as you like.' Now Roy could talk a lot of shit, but what he said caught my imagination. Nightwear for women was pretty limited. Women's dressing gowns were traditional chunky affairs, often pink and fluffy and matching the bedroom slippers. Here was something simple but sophisticated. Nice feel on the skin. Classy and sexy, but probably cheap to buy. We thumbed through a trade directory and found a clothing manufacturer in Singapore. They could make kimonos for us but the minimum order was 2,500 at a cost of £3,000. Roy looked at me and nodded eagerly, which was fine for him as he had no money and would therefore be making no financial contribution to the venture. I sent the Singapore company a telex confirming the order and a banker's draft by post to follow.

The delivery time was to be six weeks so Roy and I used this period to set ourselves up in business. We formed a limited company and imaginatively called it RoyHawk. We took an office in Ewell

Village just outside Epsom and installed two desks, two telephones, a telex machine and a filing cabinet. During the last couple of weeks before the delivery we sat opposite one another smiling. Sometimes to ease his boredom Roy would ring me up.

Finally the phone did ring and it wasn't Roy. It was our freight agent informing us that our goods had arrived at Heathrow Airport and as soon as they had been cleared by Customs we could collect them from the freight sheds. We awaited his return call.

Instead, about two hours later, our front door was kicked in – this was highly unnecessary as it was ajar – and two burly men burst into our little office. I thought it might have been John Thaw and Dennis Waterman but they announced themselves as Customs and Excise officers.

'Are you RoyHawk Ltd?'

'I'm Roy, he's Hawk,' said Roy standing up and trying to shake the men's hands.

'Are you the directors of RoyHawk Ltd?'

'We certainly are,' said Roy. I was still speechless. 'And how can we help you gentlemen?'

'We are arresting you for importing goods without a licence and said goods are being impounded under Section . . .'

The officer who wasn't reading from the statute book started to look around the office and began opening the drawers in the filing cabinet. Three were empty and the other contained a tie that Roy kept for emergencies. This seemed to deepen their suspicion of us and they told us that we would have to accompany them back to their interview suite at Heathrow Airport.

'Can I fetch our lawyer? He's only ten minutes away,' I pleaded and the two men agreed. I didn't have a lawyer – as yet I hadn't needed one – but I drove into Epsom and walked into the first solicitor's office I could find. It was half an hour before anyone could see me and I was told how irregular it was to see a customer without an appointment. The old boy was so ancient I thought he may have helped with the drafting of the Magna Carta, but after I explained the situation and he flicked through some dusty old reference books, he finally agreed to come with me to see the Customs men.

When we arrived back at the office, there was a note pinned to the door from Roy saying simply 'IN THE LOOSE BOX'. The Loose Box was a pub on the corner of the crossroads in the village that was trying to transform itself into a trendy wine bar. Roy was sitting at a table with the Customs men and I could see they were into their third bottle of Liebfraumilch. This was looking good. I bought a fourth and two more glasses and joined them. To my amazement Roy had reached Christian name and arm-round-the-shoulder terms with them in the space of an hour. When one of the Customs men bought a bottle, I knew then we were fine. We all walked back to the office and the senior Customs man phoned his office and arranged for us to be issued with the relevant licences and for our goods to be released. We saw them out and even persuaded them to drop a now heavily bemused elderly solicitor back in Epsom on their way home. My method of payment – a £10 note tucked into his breast pocket – was obviously not what he was accustomed to.

Our empty office was soon full when we unloaded the boxes of kimonos. They looked and felt exquisite but 2,500 of the fuckers fazed me a bit.

'Do you really think we can knock this lot out, Roy?'

'No problem, Philipo. We knock them out at three quid, the shops knock them out at a fiver. These are luxury items these are.'

Give the man his due. Roy was out on the road next day and somehow got Harvey Nichols, Biba, Harrods and any other shop he visited in the vicinity to take some. On that first day he got rid of about 200.

'What do we have to do now, invoice them?'

'Not yet, Phil.' Roy then explained he hadn't actually sold any kimonos but had given ten each to all the shops that would take them on a trial sale-or-return basis. He saw my shoulders deflate.

'Don't worry, Philip, we have to accumulate to speculate.'

'Speculate to accumulate, Roy.'

'That's it.'

The phone didn't ring. Even though I sat there willing it to. All week Roy was out in the car dishing out the samples. I stopped him when he had distributed 500 of the 2,500 without getting a penny back. Finally, ten days after delivery, the phone rang and I let it go two or three times so as not to appear desperate.

'Hello, is that RoyHawk?'

'Yes, can I help you?'

'Hi, my name is Davina, I'm chief buyer for Biba.'

'Oh, yes.' Stay calm Philip.

'We had one of your nice chaps in here last week with some kimonos. Actually they've gone very well, you know. We've sold all the ones we took. Ten, I believe. We'd like to order ten dozen.'

Bingo! We were in business. The next day Harrods put in an order and within a month we had sold out of our first consignment. Roy reckons Harrods were knocking them out at fifteen quid!

I got on to the Singapore factory and ordered 10,000 units, expressing my satisfaction with the first consignment. They agreed a price of £10,000 and this time gave me 30 days to pay. We almost had enough from the first batch anyway but I knew we'd sell enough in the 30 days to cover ourselves. And so what if things went wrong? We were a limited company with limited liability of £100. We couldn't lose.

Sales went from strength to strength. We couldn't get in at Marks & Spencer but every two-bit boutique and all the more broad-minded stores were buying from us. Or Roy to be exact. One clothes shop in Worthing of all places was selling ten a week. Was there no end to the British public's hunger for kimonos? This continued into the hot summer of 1976. I had my dream now. A business. A product. And all the trappings. I bought a Jaguar XJ6 and Roy predictably splashed out on a Mustang convertible. He was in his element. This was Roy Dean at his peak. The sun beating down. Shirt off. Draped across his car with 'Tonight's the Night' rasped by Rod Stewart on the eight-track as he winked at the young girls passing by.

RoyHawk was a fast-growing business, albeit a one-trick pony. We employed a receptionist, Marina, and that allowed me the opportunity to get out of the office and spend some of my money. The supplier in Singapore must have loved us and I rather fancied we had become their biggest customer, as they invited us to visit them. At the same time I was contacted by the Singapore Trade Commission in London who had got to hear about us and claimed we were among the British companies doing the most trade with their country. It was pretty heady stuff and they wanted to give us some publicity. Tempting as it was I turned this down and neglected to tell Roy. He would have jumped at the chance of a feature article with colour pictures of him everywhere being hailed as a thrusting young businessman, but I didn't want anyone else jumping on the kimono bandwagon.

We were also contacted by a man called Paul Elisha, who, because of the timing, I assumed had been put on to us by the Singapore Trade Commission. Elisha offered to accompany us to Singapore when we visited our suppliers. He asked permission to use our phones and our telex machine, which I thought was a bit weird, but he seemed a nice enough man and I thought his contacts in Singapore might prove useful.

As it happened, his contacts in Singapore might have proved fatal. On the plane over, first class of course, Elisha commented nonchalantly, 'I might have trouble getting in.'

He went on to explain that, although he had a big following in Singapore, he had been thrown out of the country some years earlier when he had stood against the Prime Minister Lee Kuan Yew in some elections. He and Lee Kuan Yew were enemies, he claimed, although they had been educated in England together. He was returning to Singapore to resurrect his political career and was bringing us over as examples of foreign trade he could bring to the country. All the late-night calls and telexes in our office had been him orchestrating his return. Now he tells us. I looked over at Roy, clueless, the spearhead of British trade, knocking back another gin and tonic and restraining himself from patting the hostess's arse as she passed him in the aisle.

At Singapore Airport we were rushed through customs, bundled politely into a waiting limo and driven at speed to our hotel. The day before I had been eating egg and chips in the greasy spoon below the office; now I was being treated like royalty in a foreign land. Elisha was receiving one visitor after another and it was clear he was who he said he was. I didn't fancy being in his shoes. Singapore is a democracy in name only, he told me. Funny things happen in Singapore, he kept saying. You can go to prison for spitting in the street. (I passed that one on to Roy.) People can disappear. Why come back then, you fucking idiot, I thought. We didn't see much of him after the first day as he obviously had bigger fish to fry, but shortly before our return home he came to the hotel with a man who owned an electronics factory.

Elisha explained his vision. 'The future is in mobile telecommunications. One day everyone will carry their own telephone on their person. We will all have our own personal telephone numbers and we should think hard about being the first in there. With your contacts and business ability and our factories and know-how we can make millions.'

Roy and I tried to suppress our laughter. The contacts and business ability bit was amusing enough but the notion of people carrying telephones on their person was ridiculous. This was 1976 – the video recorder hadn't even been invented. Where would they put these telephones anyway? The receiver tied around the neck and the bit you dial from under the arm? To us it seemed incomprehensible.

'Where would you plug them in, Paul?' asked Roy.

'They'd run on the same principle as the wireless.'

'I see,' nodded Roy, who saw nothing. The thing about Roy and I was, we knew a good idea when we saw one.

Our suppliers were the most gracious hosts, showing us around their factory during the day, embarrassing us in the process by having every single employee bow to us as we passed them, and entertaining us lavishly at night. We were supplied with drink, food and beautiful girls. Who could ask for more? When we returned home, it was without Elisha; he stayed on to consolidate his position as a political alternative to Lee Kuan Yew. I have never seen or heard of him since.

Part Three

THE MIDDLE

MR MARKS: NICE MAN
– NEW YORK, USA

When Tony, my brother, came to see me after he was released from prison, he appeared to be clean. He certainly wasn't suffering from headaches.

'There's someone I know I think you should meet,' he told me 'he's like you, Phil – a real businessman. When I told him what you did, he was very interested.' Knowing what I know now, I bet he fucking was.

We went to a pub called The Red House off the Kings Road in fashionable Chelsea. Tony said, 'Howard, this is Phil. Phil, this is Howard.'

Howard Marks greeted me warmly in a distinctive, almost musical Welsh lilt. He looked like a typical overgrown student. Woolly jumper with holes in the elbows, loose jeans and sheepskin moccasin shoes. French cigarettes. His hair was long and tousled but not too long. Like he knew he had to be part of the conventional adult world but couldn't quite leave the badges of studenthood behind. London was full of these people at the time. He moved slowly and almost gracefully and exuded the quiet detachment and inner peace of someone that had smoked a lot of dope. He had. What I didn't know then (but he revealed gradually) was that Howard was already an international man of mystery and had featured on the front page of the tabloids a few years earlier as a drug-smuggling fugitive with connections to the IRA and the Mafia. To me he came across as more Austin 1100 than Austin Powers. In fact, by the time of this meeting Howard had already been through a number of identities; he told me to call him Albi but would soon adopt the persona of Mr Donald Nice.

We got on like a house on fire. Despite our different backgrounds, we connected well. Howard went to Oxford. I went to Margate. Once. Howard knew everyone. I knew Roy. He had connections in the music world, to some band called Soft Machine that I had heard of but never heard. Thankfully. If anyone else had shared with me the personal history that Howard did, I would have excused myself from the deluded person's company sharpish. But I knew it was all true. He was an extraordinary man masquerading as a very ordinary one.

About the same time, Richard Branson was creeping up on the establishment unnoticed in a similar way as he began to build up his Virgin empire, though, of course, his empire was legitimate. Lord King, former chairman of British Airways, famously remarked that his biggest mistake was underestimating Branson because of his long hair, beard and baggy jumpers.

Howard was particularly enthusiastic about the trade links RoyHawk had developed in the Far East and expounded about the potential of importing goods from these low-cost countries. He asked if he could come down and see the offices in Ewell; I told him there wasn't a lot to see but he was not deterred.

I think it was on his first visit to the desk and filing cabinet that he suggested our first business venture. 'Bureaus, Phil. We act as a private receiving address for people and companies. Like having a box number at the GPO except we don't ask any questions. We could also offer other services like telephone answering, letterheads, use of telex and so on. I really think there is a demand out there for confidential business services.'

Roy was picking at a bit of hard skin on his finger. This 'big idea' was a trifle on the boring side for him.

'Confidential business services,' Howard mused. 'Confidential

Business Services. That's what we call it: CBS. That'll piss off the record company.'

Oh, yeah, they'll be mortified, I thought.

'Not sure about that, Howard, but it sounds good to me. How do we get the customers?'

'Simple. Classified ads in *Private Eye* and *Time Out*. That'll be a start.'

To me they seemed an odd choice of media in which to advertise a corporate service, but Howard was right. (Had he done this before?) From the first couple of ads we signed up 60 or 70 customers and again I was rubbing my hands. This was so easy. A couple of hundred quid a shot just for receiving post and the occasional telex. I had visions of building up our client list to 600 or 6,000 or even 60,000 customers. All we had to do was step up the advertising.

The strangest people came to pick up the letters and packages or to collect a telex. Parcels arrived from India, Japan, China, Jamaica and almost every other part of the world. Howard collected quite a few himself. It did occur to me that some of these Jiffy bags might contain illegal substances but if they did they were pathetically small amounts so I was not perturbed. Howard's stuff was mainly letters though. He seemed to know people in a lot of different countries and we talked often about business ideas. It was soon apparent that beneath his fairly languid demeanour Howard was as sharp as a knife.

'Ever thought about doing business in Afghanistan?' he asked one afternoon as he inhaled on a Gitane.

'Not really.' Then I thought about it. 'Although I suppose we could probably start importing Afghan coats.' I was half-joking. Afghan coats had been popular with hippies for a few years now, though I suspected most were not manufactured in Afghanistan.

'Nice one,' smiled Howard. 'How about you go out there and let's see if we can start bringing in some genuine Afghan-made coats. I'll put up £8,000. You can pay me back when you've sold them.'

This seemed extraordinarily generous but I was not about to turn him down. I rather suspected that he might ask for some piece of the action or even a partnership at a later date but I'd cross that bridge when I came to it. He was inspiring and exciting. I knew Roy and I were being groomed by Howard but felt that I was capable of keeping one step ahead of him. He was about to use me and I was about to use him. Already Roy and I were beginning to believe that we could have a go at anything and make money, and Howard just added to the general feeling that anything was within our reach.

'How do you fancy going to Afghanistan and bringing back some coats?' I said to Roy when he returned to the office.

'No problem,' he said, but I knew he was confusing Afghanistan with Aberfan or Aberystwyth and thought I was suggesting a drive over the Severn Bridge to Wales.

We packed Roy off to the airport and he got a flight to Kabul. I think that took some doing. Then people only wanted to leave Afghanistan. I suspect they still do. He managed to source some lovely Afghan coats and £8,000-worth were soon winging their way over to Heathrow. The coats arrived back before Roy did and he seemed to have enjoyed the trip, saying he had made a few friends there.

Meanwhile, Howard had moved to New York and was only flying back into London intermittently. When he did, he called and I would go to meet him at the Devonshire Hotel, where I would pass over his mail from the office and he would bung me some money for expenses. He was delighted that the coats were going well. Not in the same numbers as the kimonos but we had a great margin on them.

RoyHawk had also decided to diversify before Howard's arrival in our lives and we had reinvested some of our burgeoning profits into a bright-yellow breakdown recovery vehicle. We had a vision of breaking the monopoly of the AA and the RAC. Direct Line and Green Flag have done it since, but properly. I'm not sure where this idea came from. It was probably me and I have tried to erase all memory of it from my mind. We hired, headhunted even, a mechanic acquaintance of ours called Geoff and he brought along Tom, his mate. We had the vehicle sign written and placed a few ads. They couldn't believe their luck as they were on better wages and went from not doing much work at all to not doing any. They sometimes went out in the truck looking for accidents but I would pass it many times during the day parked outside The Wellington pub in Epsom.

One day Howard called me and asked if I would fly out to New York to meet him. He had had an idea. He told me it involved the opportunity to earn a large amount of money. I deduced that drugs of some sort figured in this idea. He seemed to have become quite rich and was basing himself out in the Big Apple. I wasn't going to miss the opportunity of visiting America so I didn't hang about. Howard had suggested I bring Roy with me but as Roy was hunting Afghan coats in Kabul I asked Geoff, the breakdown man, if he wanted to come.

'Do you own a passport, Geoff?'

Surprisingly he did. He might have been to Benidorm but I doubted it – he struck me as the sort of bloke that started to get homesick if he got beyond Dorking.

'Want to come to New York with me? I've got to see someone and might need help with some bits and pieces.'

Geoff was nodding enthusiastically.

A few hours later we were on Freddie Laker's SkyTrain for 50 notes each on the way to the US of A. Coincidentally, Freddie Laker had horses in training at Epsom and when British Airways finally shafted his little airline he was in The Wellington pub in Epsom drowning his sorrows. For a joke, old Tommy Poulton passed around his trilby hat among the customers for Freddie's benefit.

Howard met us in style at the airport. He was sitting in the back of a huge black limousine and a huge black man was acting as his chauffeur and bodyguard. He took us on a tour of the city and we both sat transfixed as the landmarks and backdrops we knew so well from years of American films and television came to life. People really did say, 'Have a nice day.' 'Walk' and 'Don't Walk' signs flashed on every corner and the distinctive New York smell, mingled with smoke emitted from vents and pipes on the pavements, was ever present. Most of all it was the people: all sizes and colours. So many of them, all going somewhere fast. So very fast.

Howard took us up on a helicopter tour and we buzzed around the Empire State Building and between the Twin Towers like a huge metal bumblebee. He had literally swept us off our feet. I can only recall feeling similarly excited when Mum and Dad took me to Battersea Funfair as a young kid in the 1950s. We were put up in the best New York hotel and that night ate the best food.

The next day Howard got down to business.

'Do you think Roy could get 500 kilos of dope together and get it shipped to here in New York?'

'I think so,' I replied without hesitation. The terms he outlined were mouthwatering. Howard flicked open a briefcase that contained $275,000 in bundles of dollar bills. This was more money than I had ever seen. The closest I'd come to this was Monopoly money. Howard wanted us to take the cash to Frankfurt where we were to meet Roy, who was to collect it from there and take it to Kabul for the eventual purchase of the 500 kilos of Afghan puff. Howard suggested that Geoff carry the money into Frankfurt and that I travel separately, saying that I was too valuable to the operation to risk getting nicked carrying such a large amount of cash. I spoke to Geoff, and as I detailed the proposition to him I watched his Adam's apple rise and fall. I explained that if he was apprehended he should say he found the briefcase in his hotel room and panicked and took a flight to Frankfurt. It wasn't particularly convincing and Geoff knew this but the £5,000 I told him he would receive at the end just about convinced him. This represented a year's wages for Geoff. He didn't ask and I didn't tell him what was going down but the guy wasn't stupid. The only way he could deal with it was by not knowing what was happening after Frankfurt. He just wanted reassurance he could go home then.

£100,000 for me, £50,000 for Roy: this was the deal. We were talking here about more money in one hit than RoyHawk would generate in a couple of years and we were doing well by anybody's standards. I did not wrestle too much with the possible downside of getting involved in a drugs deal of this scale. If caught, even as a first offender, I would be in serious trouble and certainly face a chunky term of imprisonment. I might even have to serve it in America or some other less hospitable country. There was a small chance I could end up getting shot. But, of course, I didn't look at it like that. My youthful arrogance combined with my success in business so far, despite sailing close to the wind, caused me to discount the possibility of getting caught. Howard was a gentleman and I was convinced that he was his own boss and not involved with gangsters in any way. If I had thought for one minute I was treading on the toes of London criminals or the Mafia, I would not have gone near it, but I was safe enough. On that score I felt comfortable about what I was getting us into.

I had no qualms either about the morality of what I was about to do. I'm not sure I even thought about it at the time but I have certainly had the opportunity to do so since. Howard liked to justify his activities by describing them as the 'transportation of beneficial herbs'. He dressed it up a little in a cloak of protest by anti-establishment people against silly legislation. He saw himself, or wanted others to see him, in the same light as the hippies behind *Oz* magazine, who were imprisoned for publishing indecent material, or Mick Jagger and Keith Richards, who were banged up briefly for smoking hash. The reality was that Howard was in the business of the transportation of money beneficial to Howard. Having said that, his business was built on charm and trust, not violence and intimidation like most other criminal empires, and he never succumbed to the temptation of transporting hard drugs such as cocaine or heroin around the globe. Not even he could claim these latter substances were beneficial.

I had never smoked dope of any kind. At that point I would not have known the difference between a Thai stick and a lolly stick. Therefore, unlike Howard, I could not confirm or deny the beneficial effects of smoking this stuff. What I did know was that I had never seen people smashing up a bar or ramming glasses into each other's faces after smoking a joint. I had seen it enough times over the years after they had drunk six pints of lager, yet lager was legal. It still is. From personal observation it was clear that dope was more likely to calm people down than provoke them into violence or a life of crime. Grass was a natural substance; it came from the ground. Like homosexuality or gambling, I believed that it would be legalised sooner or later and, meanwhile, if governments were going to be stupid enough to prohibit something that large numbers of their populations wanted to indulge in, I would try to benefit from their short-sightedness.

There are downsides to dope smoking. Excessive use can lead to extreme lethargy. I know people who smoke a great deal and have lost the will to work. The really bad ones have lost the will to get out of bed. But excessive drinking leads to unconsciousness. Regular excessive drinking leads to liver problems and death. Why is one drug legal and not the other? I am not an apologist for dope – as I say, it has never interested me as a leisure pursuit – but the inconsistency rankles. Ban them both by all means.

History will show that the reason dope was banned for so long and a smuggling industry grew up around it is that dope was the preferred drug of young people. Political and economic power was concentrated in the hands of older people whose preferred drug was alcohol. Only when the young people grew older and the power passed to them did the possibility of dope becoming legal start to emerge. These once-young people and recreational dope smokers were still alive despite their use of this 'evil substance': some were running multinational companies, some were in the Cabinet, some were among the richest musicians and film stars in the world, the rest were all over the globe leading normal lives that included, even in late middle age, smoking a few joints when they fancied it.

Grass, dope, puff, blow, draw, pot, hash, waccy-baccy − call it what you will, it has been grown, cultivated and inhaled or eaten since the earliest of times. Many people believe there are references to it in the Bible (whoever wrote the Old Testament must have been on something). The undoubted medicinal benefits have been recognised for centuries and are currently, as the latest wave of paranoia subsides, being acknowledged and researched again. There is a company quoted on the London Stock Exchange devoted to developing the commercial possibilities of cannabis in this area. But the bad press the drug has received also goes back a long way. In the Middle Ages, people believed that it was a major ingredient of witches' brews and helped them fly around the countryside on their broomsticks. It gained popularity in Europe, though, when Napoleon's army got stuck in Egypt and their soldiers sampled the cannabis-based hubbly-bubbly pipe and delightedly brought their new leisure pursuit home with them. The Parisian in-crowd seized upon the drug, believing it inspired their creativity. Its use spread around nineteenth-century Europe among the arty-farty crowd.

Even the Americans caught on and cannabis use was initially neither illegal nor frowned upon. On the contrary, leading confectioners even produced cannabis candy throughout the mid-nineteenth century. Across the Atlantic, when Lewis Carroll's *Alice in Wonderland* was released, no eyebrows were raised at the dope-smoking caterpillar; caterpillars were like that. The tide, however, turned early in the twentieth century when jazz music first showed signs of being embraced by the white majority in America. Jazz musicians, and black jazz musicians in particular, had made no secret of their pastime. Reactionary Americans, fearful of the white race becoming contaminated by blacks, demonised the drug and held it up as an example of the disgusting way of life practised by these jazz lovers. Like alcohol before it, grass was banned. The taste for alcohol was so widespread and strong that the prohibition on it had to be lifted, but because cannabis was an acquired taste with low penetration of the population in terms of usage, common sense did not prevail. A small industry sprang up, circumventing the law and supplying the demand that remained. The shit really hit the fan, though, when all-American boys went to war in Vietnam and returned home a few years later with a penchant for smoking grass. Suddenly and unexpectedly the drug showed signs of becoming mainstream. It thus got lumped in with heroin and other hard and genuinely dangerous drugs, and war was declared on the people trafficking in it and, in extreme cases, the countries growing it. Now was the time for the really sensible people to keep their heads down. I was never really sensible.

Howard booked me on to Concorde for my Frankfurt trip and I could have sworn I passed Geoff in the air – in the window seat of his plane, sitting bolt upright with sweat pouring off his brow and his eyes bulging. At the hotel I waited in the bar for Roy, who soon bounced in all back-slaps and smiles. I told him the whole story and he was not the slightest bit fazed.

'It's a lot of money you will be taking into Kabul, Roy. It's a big deal. It's very dangerous. If you get caught you could get shot, or thrown into prison.'

'This calls for champagne. Barman!'

Roy was confident he could set the deal up and carry it off. He said he knew anyone that was anyone in Kabul. This was possibly true. We decided to go out on the town to celebrate our good fortune. I went up in the lift to fetch Geoff, who was alone in his room with a briefcase full of money and had not yet joined us in the bar. I knocked on his door but he would not let me in. I could hear him crying though.

'What's the matter, Geoff?'

'Go away,' he wailed, 'I'm not coming out.' He was talking some unintelligible nonsense and was mentioning the money, the briefcase, Howard and Roy. Geoff was clearly traumatised. I went back downstairs and told Roy.

'What's his room number?' he asked. Unbeknown to me, Roy

then went upstairs and somehow gained access to the room next door to Geoff and went out on to the balcony. Six floors up, he climbed over to the balcony of Geoff's room and burst open his French windows.

'Batman!' he announced. This did nothing for Geoff's delicate frame of mind. Roy took the case and we booked Geoff on the next plane home. He trembled all the way to the airport. Not surprisingly he didn't come back to work for RoyHawk. He didn't need to with his £5,000 but we heard later that he had been arrested back home for a pretty silly offence. I like to think there were some problems there already and our escapade wasn't the root of his troubles but I have to confess that walking through Frankfurt Airport with over a quarter of a million dollars in a briefcase probably caused the breakdown man to break down.

The next morning Roy and the briefcase were on an Ariana Airways flight to Kabul. I travelled back to New York to see Howard and sort out exactly how the load would be shipped to New York. I worried about Roy. The average wage in Afghanistan, if you were fortunate enough to have a job, was $3 a week. If the case inadvertently fell open on a Kabul street there would have been weeks of street riots. Plenty of people would have quite happily shot him for the kind of money he was bringing in. And I'm not talking about bandits and guerillas here. Imagine a couple of Afghan customs officers being faced with a briefcase stuffed with $275,000. It would have been very tempting to bundle Roy outside and kill him.

After nearly a week without word from Roy, my concerns increased and Howard suggested that I travel out to Kabul to see how he was getting on. After I had booked my flight, Roy made contact by telex and said he had set everything up. I asked him to meet me at the airport and urged him to be discreet. I was anxious we should do nothing now to draw attention to ourselves.

My plane landed in Kabul at five in the morning. There were only a handful of other passengers on the small 120-seater plane. The airport would not have been able to cope with anything larger. The other travellers were either locals or English or American hippies visiting the land of the drug they worshipped. I had $5,000 in my pocket to cover any extra expenses that may have occurred or would occur. The airport was little more than a shed with a tin roof on it and as I passed through 'Customs' I exchanged $100 at the exchange counter. These days we have hole-in-the-wall machines; well, this really was a hole crudely punched into the wall. The rates being offered were scribbled up on a blackboard in chalk. A man that I vaguely recognised as an extra from *Carry on Up the Khyber* handed me a wad of notes that I hurriedly stuffed into a carrier bag. A little man hopped over to me as I hit the fresh air and took me unawares by snatching the bag from my hand. He wasn't running away so I realised he wasn't a thief but maybe some kind of porter. I caught up with him by the taxi rank and took the bag back, reaching in and giving him a handful of notes. The little man whooped with delight and this stirred the taxi-drivers, who up until then had been slouched back in their seats dozing. Before I knew it the drivers had surrounded the man and were furiously trying to snatch the notes from him. Then it started to turn nasty as the drivers exchanged blows. Obviously I had overtipped. I think I had handed over about three months' wages. Stupid. Very stupid. Where the fuck was Roy?

A massive soft-top American Cadillac pulled up alongside. There was Roy, grinning broadly in sunglasses even though the sun had not yet risen.

'Hop in, old son.'

I asked him where he had got the car.

'It belongs to the Crown Prince of Afghanistan,' he explained casually. 'I met him at the Supper Club on the top floor of the Intercontinental Hotel. He loves me, Phil. Lent me the motor. Phil, you should see the women he has in tow.'

Roy rolled his eyes and licked his lips. I dreaded to think what he had been up to. I thought that if this was Roy's idea of being discreet and keeping a low profile, I'd hate to see what he would do if he were asked to make himself known. As we passed through the streets of Kabul, policemen, or perhaps soldiers, standing on street corners saluted us as they recognised the royal car. Roy returned the acknowledgement with a blast on the car's ridiculous air horns that, believe it or not, played the tune of 'Colonel Bogie'.

'For fuck's sake Roy,' I sighed as I slid down in the passenger seat. He said he had told the Crown Prince he was interested in setting up a factory in Kabul and was trying to get a feel for the place. He whipped up the Prince's enthusiasm by saying he thought Afghanistan was the next Singapore.

We went straight to a warehouse in Chicken Street, where Roy couldn't wait to show me 500 kilos of the finest Afghan hash.

'Only me,' shouted Roy as we eased ourselves in the door. A couple of Afghans with large rifles slung over their shoulders approached us.

'This is John,' he said pointing at me. 'He big boss.'

Thanks Roy. I felt like the man from Del Monte as I cut off a lump from one of the boxes and burnt it. This was what Howard told me to do and the odour was strong. Preferably he would have liked me to smoke some but Roy had and assured me it was 'good gear'.

'We'll take it,' I said. Smiles all round and everyone in the warehouse was nodding at each other. I then spent some time trying to explain how we needed the hash wrapped and packed into wooden crates and that exact shipping details would follow.

After leaving the warehouse we made our way through the city back to the hotel. The streets of Kabul were little more than mud tracks with shacks, shops and shanty houses running along each side. I noticed a series of butcher shops displaying their carcasses and meat hanging from hooks outside. They like their meat well done over here, I thought, looking at the jet-black colour of the offerings. But as any potential customers approached, the shopkeeper would scurry out of the shop and clap his hands loudly, at which the flies would fly off the meat to reveal the real colour of the flesh.

Later that afternoon, as I did a bit of exploring around Kabul, I had the upsetting experience of being a spectator as a man was killed. There were no pavements in the city and I had quickly learned not to expect any vehicle to have any regard for anyone walking in the road. A team of single-decker buses that must have been manufactured in the 1930s sped around the streets carrying twice as many passengers as they had been built to cope with. I caught sight of these buses hurtling down a hill towards me and stepped back into the safety of a shop doorway, but an elderly and rather frail-looking Afghan man in front of me decided to try and make it to the other side of the road. He didn't. The bus driver either did not see him or did not bother to apply his brakes. The old man was knocked up in the air and landed at the side of the road. The coach stopped and the driver got out, as did the hundred or so people on the bus, and they crowded around the prostrate body. When they had decided he was dead, they all reboarded and carried on their journey. The man was left at the side of the road like a dead fox.

When I told Roy about it back at the hotel he was nonchalant.

'They're all fucking mad down there. I try and stay at the hotel,' he said. The Intercontinental stood majestically on a hill overlooking Kabul and I wondered who would be patronising such a posh hotel in such a poor country. The guests seemed to be a mixture of American and Russian diplomats and a selection of charity workers and do-gooders obviously being very careful with their particular country's foreign aid. The Yanks and the Russians were competing at the time to throw aid at Afghanistan. For the Russians the country had great strategic importance in the region and would give them access to a warm water port. The Americans just didn't want the Russians to have it.

Outside Kabul the Russian aid manifested itself in the construction of large roads heading out of Kabul and over to the Russian border. I wondered why they didn't throw the money at building proper roads and a decent infrastructure for the capital. These country roads going nowhere were big enough to drive a tank down. A few years later that was exactly what the Russians did when they invaded.

That first night Roy drove me out to a small village for a 'night out'. It turned out to be a dogfight. The dogs were pit bull terriers; they had had their tails and ears removed so there was nothing for the other dog to cling to. Money was changing hands and I was told that if only a small amount of money had been wagered then the fight would be stopped when one dog was clearly winning, both owners not wishing to lose their own dog. But, if large amounts had been staked, then the fight would be to the death, because the owner would want to ensure he got the prize money. I didn't fancy hanging around to see what type of bout this one was to be.

The following evening, still on a high over the imminent deal and the prospect of serious personal enrichment, Roy told me we had been invited to a reception at the American Embassy. Whatever next with this man? Dogfight one day, Ambassador's party the next. Nowadays when I see the television advert where the ambassador hands out the chocolates, it reminds me of this evening. I suggested I better go into town and find a dress-hire shop.

'Do you honestly think there is a fucking Moss Bros in downtown Kabul? You're having a laugh.' He persuaded me that the creased cotton John Collier suit I had travelled in would be fine. But when Roy met me in the hotel reception, he had really gone to town. He wore a white jacket and white heavily flared trousers. Under his jacket was a frilly red Bobby Crush shirt and under his shirt gold medallions galore competed with one another for attention. A red silk handkerchief in his breast pocket set it all off. His hair was already permed. Roy was a tall man but the platform shoes he was wearing made him tower above me. This truly was Roy's John Travolta from *Saturday Night Fever* phase. He was like the most flamboyant male clothes model ever and next to him I felt like the clothes shop stock-taker and back-room clerk.

At the embassy building we were waved through into a large reception room where anyone who was anyone in expatriate

Afghanistan was gathered, standing around as butlers filled their champagne glasses.

'Hello, Roy,' smiled various women as we squeezed our way through the room.

'Told you Phil, wall-to-wall cunt. If we don't get our nuts tonight then I'm a Chinaman.'

I was amazed at the people he had got to know in such a short time and more amazed by the impression he had already made. Our arrival seemed to cause more than just a ripple of interest and people eagerly pressed their hands into ours. One man was a caricature Englishman. His extraordinary handlebar moustache bristled as he greeted us with, 'Glad you could make it old chaps.' Roy said he was the captain of the Queen's flight.

Two pretty young English girls spoke to us.

'Missionaries. Absolutely gagging for it,' Roy whispered in my ear whilst I tried to conduct a sensible conversation with them. Then he cocked his leg slightly and grinned knowingly. I knew he was squeezing out a sly fart, just as he would have done back in the school classroom. I recoiled a bit as the smell hit me almost immediately and noticed that Roy had raised his eyebrows to me in a meaningful way.

'Quick, let's fuck off,' he hissed.

'Why, what's up?'

'I've shit myself. I've followed through. Cover my back as we walk out,' he pleaded.

I took up position behind him and could not suppress my laughter as he headed for the door. More people were trying to stop him and engage him in conversation but a very noticeable and expanding brown stain had appeared on the seat of Roy's white trousers and was travelling down one leg fast. This remains one of the favourite memories of my entire life.

With everything in order, save Roy's bowel movements, I left him to it in Kabul and returned to the office in Ewell. He was to receive final transportation instructions direct from Howard and then come home. On safe arrival of the hash in New York, Howard was to weigh us on. I couldn't help fantasising about the money coming my way. It was enough for three decent houses in Epsom; or I could have bought Jimmy Greaves, the footballer. Mind you, if I had bought him I'm not sure what I would have done with him, what with his drinking and all that. But what really excited me was the fact that Howard had indicated there was plenty more where that came from. My greed was almost tangible.

'Where the fuck is that nutter?' I had never heard Howard angry before.

He was on the phone one evening telling me that Roy was not contactable. The dope had not arrived as arranged and Roy was not responding to telexes or phone calls. At the same time I was getting grief from Roy's girlfriend. Because of my reticence and because my story as to Roy's whereabouts was not adding up she thought I had killed him for a full share of RoyHawk's profits.

'There's something not right here, Phil. If I haven't heard from Roy by the end of the week, I'm going to the police. He's been missing six weeks now.'

Things were spiralling out of control. I didn't need the police investigating Roy's suspected murder and looking into our affairs. Frighteningly, though, there was a possibility that Roy *had* been murdered. I took the next flight to Kabul to find out what on earth was going on. The lady at the desk at the Intercontinental Hotel confirmed he had checked out nearly three weeks earlier. My stomach somersaulted. I decided not to ask my armed friends in the warehouse if they knew what had happened to him. I went back to the airport and after bunging them wads of dollars, I was able to discover that he had bought a one-way ticket to Singapore via Dubai. I should have guessed – Singapore being the only other country in the world besides England and Spain that Roy had ever visited. I caught the next plane to Singapore.

Where to start? He was not booked into the hotel we had stayed at last time. Next I thought there was a chance he might be visiting the nightclubs on Orchard Street that we had had so much fun in with our kimono hosts. The first one I went in was the 394 Club and I sat in a table by the corner of the stage, racking my brains for a plan of action to find Roy. I was severely depressed. It didn't add up but there seemed no other conclusion – my friend and partner had done a runner with $275,000. Why wait so long though? Why go through the whole charade of setting up the deal and making even more potential enemies along the way? Why not fuck off the first day he and the briefcase were alone together? It didn't add up. As I was turning all these thoughts over in my mind and sipping my beer, my eyes were jolted to the stage by the compère's introduction: 'And all the way from London, England's very own Frank Sinatra. Ladies and gentlemen, please put your hands together for Mr Roy Dean.'

From behind the velvet curtain he stepped, clutching his microphone and launching into 'My Way'. You certainly fucking did, I thought, as the spotlight illuminated his grinning face. His set was mercifully short, as he could not sing to save his life, so I stood up and made myself known to him as he waited for the calls for an encore that were not forthcoming. We went backstage.

'I'm sorry, mate,' he said as he looked down at the floor.

'You're fucking sorry. What's going on? Have you cracked up like Geoff?'

'No. No. I just couldn't face you or Howard. I knew you wouldn't believe me.'

'Believe you, Roy? What have you done?'

'Well, I got invited to go horse-riding up in the Hindu Kush mountains by this gorgeous bird. You should have seen her, Phil – tits like rockets, and I was sort of worried about leaving the cash in my room all day, especially as I was banking on not coming back that night, so I gave it to one of the waiters to look after. He was my mate, this bloke, I'd been tipping him well and we got along great. It didn't occur to me he'd nick it.'

'You gave a waiter nearly $300,000 to look after?' I was staggered.

'He's gone, Phil. No trace of him at all.'

'Of course he's fucking gone. He's the richest waiter in the entire fucking world, isn't he?'

I told him to phone Pauline, his girlfriend, and tell her he was still alive, and advised him to get on the next plane back to England.

I decided to tell Howard the truth, the whole truth and nothing but the truth. He believed me, although he was more sceptical about Roy. Until Howard floated it, I had not considered the notion that Roy might still be turning us over. He wasn't. If he had taken that money, he would not have fled to Singapore and taken a job as a nightclub singer. I know Roy: he would have gone off on a massive spend-up. Howard thought he might have stashed the money for later use but again Roy was not that subtle and if he did – well, Roy is certainly being careful, because a quarter of a century later he still hasn't dipped into it. The only thing Roy would ever steal from his friends was their limelight.

Howard was extraordinarily pragmatic about the whole sorry business. He had not lost confidence in me, he said, and there were further deals to be done, but Roy, he insisted, was history. There were some 'angry investors' around but providing Roy did not appear again there was no threat to his personal safety. Howard also said he could not deal with me again if Roy remained my business partner.

I had decided that my immediate future lay with Howard and longer term in the transportation of beneficial herbs. With great regret, Roy and I terminated our business relationship and went our separate ways. Knowing what he knows now, Roy is, I'm sure, greatly relieved we did. We had some great laughs and went from one exciting jape to another. Our lives, for a while, were like one long episode of *Minder*. All good things come to an end though.

Meanwhile, in a penthouse flat overlooking the sea in Monte Carlo, a former Intercontinental Hotel table waiter drops to his knees five times daily and thanks Allah for his extraordinary good fortune.

FLIRTY FISHING AND MEN IN BOATS
– HONG KONG

'Fly to Hong Kong. Book into the Mandarin Hotel and wait. Someone will contact you. Enjoy yourself.' These were Howard's instructions; he had also provided me with a hefty few thousand pounds to ensure I could do just that. One drawback was that I had to leave my girlfriend Shirley behind. This was a pain, because for the first time since my failed marriage I had started to grow really fond of someone. Inevitably she too would become tired of hanging around for a bloke who was never there. Nevertheless, living like a lord in a five-star hotel in one of the world's more exotic centres eased the pain and boredom that came after the first few weeks of waiting.

Things seemed to be taking a turn for the better when, as I sat in the hotel bar bored and eavesdropping on other people's conversations one evening, a young lady made eye contact with me. She was white, with long shiny black hair and an hourglass figure to die for. She was impeccably dressed. When she stood up and headed towards me, I almost panicked. I think I may have looked over my shoulder to check there was no drop-dead gorgeous man behind me.

'Can I join you?' she asked in a husky American voice.

'By all means,' I replied, thinking she must be a prostitute. But an American prostitute working out of a posh Hong Kong hotel bar? She told me she worked for the Hong Kong and Shanghai Bank, which seemed plausible. She was single and had recently been posted here, so she was lonely. Fucking hell. I asked her if she'd like to eat and we went into town to a nice restaurant. Her name was Rachel. She was flirtatious but not overly so. A touch of the hand. A crossing of the legs. A flick of that lovely hair. When the meal ended I was unsure how to play it.

'Would you like to go to a nightclub?'

'I'd rather go to your hotel room.' Geronimo! Back at the room she stripped, displaying no signs of shyness, to reveal a beautiful body and we enjoyed probably the best sex I had had in my life up until that point. I didn't want it to stop. Her appetite for performing oral sex on me was quite shocking. In the morning, as she dressed to go back to her apartment in town before going to work, I asked whether we could meet up again.

'It would be my pleasure,' she smiled sweetly, as I watched her wiggle her little arse back into her skirt.

All day I mused on the night before. I could not get Rachel out of my mind. Silly thoughts started entering my head. Like doing some legitimate business here in Hong Kong and sharing an apartment with her. At around four in the afternoon my bedside phone rang. A female voice at the other end said she was a work colleague of Rachel's and that Rachel was sorry but she would not be able to keep our appointment tonight.

'That's a pity,' I said with forced nonchalance but my disappointment was obvious.

'If you like,' continued Rachel's friend, 'I'll come over and see you.'

'That would be nice.'

What was going on here? My head swelled. Perhaps Rachel had told her friend what a great lover I was and she wanted a piece herself behind her friend's back. What I hadn't told Rachel was that I had not had sex for a couple of months whilst hanging around the Mandarin and my stamina and enthusiasm had been partly the result of carrying a heavy load.

Rachel's friend arrived. Her name was Sarah and she was a cracker too – taller than Rachel and even taller than me but quite stunning. Every head in the bar turned when she strode in. We sat down and had a few drinks. She was from California and had also been in Hong Kong only a short time.

'Would you like to eat?' I offered.

'I've heard the food on room service is pretty good.' My penis heard this and pushed against my trousers so hard that I had to untuck my shirt in the hope of covering the bulge as we took the lift to my room. Sarah practically threw me on to the bed and took the lead in what was another energetic sex session. Like her friend, she had an unusual enthusiasm for carrying out oral sex. At some point in the night we did get room service. During a lull in the proceedings I had to ask, 'You don't know someone called Howard Marks do you?'

'No, who's he?'

'No, doesn't matter.'

In the morning, the whole experience was playing on my mind still. 'Come on then, Sarah, what's the deal? Two beautiful women hunting me down one night after the other. This doesn't happen in real life. What is going on here?'

Sarah sat back down on the bed and stroked my head like I was a child.

'Rachel and me, we're Children of God,' she said, as though this somehow explained everything.

'What, you mean you're Christians?'

'No Phil, we are in the Children of God. Our leader is David Moses and we are here to spread the word and have more children for the Children.'

I didn't want to hear any more. Sounds ridiculous, I know, but I felt used. These beautiful birds were after my money or my sperm. Possibly both. I didn't relish the thought of fathering children for some strange religious cult. Whatever next in this mad life I was leading?

I had no desire to see Rachel, Sarah or any other nutcases from the Children of God again, so I changed rooms and instructed reception to put no calls through to me from any females. I stayed out of the bar for a while too but one day in reception I was intercepted by two earnest young men dressed in black suits. They told me they were also from the Children of God (Hong Kong branch) and tried to persuade me to join with the promise of lots more like Rachel and Sarah. No thanks, I told them. Okay, but would I be prepared to donate to the church? I told them I was merely a travel agent travelling on my company's budget and I was returning home to my wife and family the following day. They were ever so polite, wished me a nice life and I never saw them again.

A few years later I was travelling first class on an aeroplane when I was handed a complimentary copy of a news magazine. The Children of God were being exposed in the magazine as a religious cult on a par with the Moonies or the mob who followed Jim Jones and committed suicide en masse in the jungle. It told of their leader David Moses' obsession with sex and hinted at child abuse, brainwashing and much more. Of particular interest to me was the description of their modus operandi. The prettiest girls among their number were selected and sent out into the big cities to recruit gullible, preferably wealthy, single men into their group. Did they mean me?

This practice was called 'flirty fishing' and, after much criticism, was finally abandoned in the late 1980s after the AIDS epidemic had taken hold. The article said that single men in international hotels were particular targets and that the Children of God themselves admitted that they had an eight out of ten success rate using this method. They justified the practice by claiming that the Bible promotes lateral thinking in discovering ways of spreading the word. The Children of God developed the 'we'll open our legs, you open your mind' approach.

David Moses was really called David Berg and he had formed the group in the late 1960s in drug-soaked California. He was a disaffected hippie and the group formed from a commune of like-minded people he joined. At about the same time, Charles Manson was charting a similar course. Manson's group was called The Family and they achieved notorious immortality when they slaughtered Sharon Tate, the pregnant young wife of the film director Roman Polanski, and some friends in 1969. Ironically, years later when trying to rebuild the image that had been destroyed by flirty fishing and other scandals, the Children of God changed their name to The Family. Their most famous convert was Jeremy Spencer, who played a mean slide-guitar with the successful British pop group Fleetwood Mac. They had recently enjoyed a rare instrumental number one hit with 'Albatross'. It is not clear whether he was a victim of flirty fishing but one day in downtown Los Angeles he disappeared. Some time later he resurfaced as a committed member of the Children of God. As far as I know, he's still with them. Fleetwood Mac were vulnerable to this type of thing. Peter Green, who formed the group (it was originally named Peter Green's Fleetwood Mac), went off his head very early on and ended up spending a chunk of his life in mental institutions, their young guitarist Danny Kirwan also succumbed to mental illness and Mick Fleetwood must have been mental to present the Brit Awards one year with Samantha Fox.

David Berg died in the 1990s. At that time I read some more press articles about him and the movement. Former members told of his strange teachings. One was that semen contained considerable nutritional benefit and should be ingested at every possible opportunity.

Flirty fishing over, I settled back into my routine of spending Howard's expenses and dreaming up ways to stave off the boredom. Fortunately, within a week of my experience with the Children of God another American bearing gifts turned up. He was a contact of Howard's who we'll call Tim Munday. He handed me a cheque for $400,000 and told me to cash it and wait to hear from Howard. I was a bit nervous about doing this but the people in the bank did not bat an eyelid. Cashing that sort of money in England without a double-barrelled name or a double-barrelled shotgun would have been nigh on impossible and likely have caused massive panic in the interbank market. Howard then told me to fly to Thailand and book into the Dusit Thani Hotel in Bangkok and wait for further instructions. I was turning into James Bond before my very eyes.

Going through customs at Bangkok was the most stressful thing I had done in my life up to that point and I started to feel a lot more sympathetic to the plight of my former breakdown driver. However, getting through was one of the best feelings of my life thus far. Pure adrenalin.

The Dusit Thani was a lovely hotel, so serene and calm and at such odds with the metropolis of Bangkok outside. I fell in love with the people immediately. Their warmth and smiling politeness, characterised by their gentle bowing and holding their hands in a praying position as they welcome you, washed over me. This gesture is known as a *wai* and I soon learnt to *wai* back. The courtesy and warmth was not at all patronising or contrived, unlike the 'Have a Nice Day and Now Fuck Off' culture I had recently witnessed in New York. For me and Thailand it was love at first sight.

Another American called Todd turned up at the Dusit Thani, where he relieved me of my suitcase and told me my work was done. I was relieved and felt that I had gone some way to repaying Howard for the Kabul catastrophe. An added bonus for me was that while I was in Thailand I stumbled on a film crew in a Patpong bar shooting some scenes. I managed to gatecrash as an extra. Look carefully next time you watch *The Deer Hunter* and don't blink. You'll see me watching a go-go dancer in the beachside bar scene. Unfortunately, further film offers were not forthcoming, although later on I did also get some extra work on the war film *Full Metal Jacket*. I didn't need the money, I just hoped that one time the director would walk past me, do a double-take and demand I was given a leading part. As I was on the run by the time of the second film, it was a particularly stupid notion.

From Bangkok I flew to Paris to see Howard, at the same time delivering an envelope with a bill of lading number and some flight details for a four-ton consignment of hash worth $4 million bound for California that Todd had asked me to pass on. All these deals going down! I wanted a piece of the action.

Howard sent me straight on to Tangier with a holdall full of money to deliver to a man called Ian in the Café de Paris. I had to carry a copy of the *Financial Times* to aid my identification. This was becoming huge fun. I felt like Alec Guinness in *Our Man in Havana*. Howard told me to vary the way I returned back to England. After a night on the tiles in Tangier I flew to Gibraltar for some sightseeing, then on to Brussels from where I finally took the boat to Folkestone.

I felt I had now repaid Howard and earned his respect and confidence. I had taken no fees for my recent courier work and was looking forward to earning some serious dough. He summoned me to his new base in Italy, where he asked me to take £25,000 sterling down to Cadiz in Spain. I was to meet a man called Roy and hand it over. Simple. On arrival I called Roy and he instructed me to meet him at the marina. He sounded very brusque.

'How will I recognise you?' he grunted.

'I have a crumpled grey suit on.'

Roy found me easily enough and he looked like he sounded. A big nautical-looking man with a large beard and grizzly grey chest hairs falling in curls out of his shirt. He took the money and then fixed his eye on me.

'Where's the rest of the crew?'

'What are you on about?' I was genuinely puzzled but Roy went berserk at me.

'You're meant to know what's happening, you little shit. You're meant to be supplying crew. I suggest you get on the phone to your guv'nor and find out what the fucking hell is going on. You hear me?'

Suddenly I felt like I was back in the headmaster's study. I went to a phone box from where I called Howard and relayed the story. In his inimitable way, Howard said, 'Would you mind, Phil? Go with Roy and be his crew. It won't take long.'

I went back to Roy who had now been joined by a chap called Bill.

'I'm the rest of your crew,' I smiled weakly, 'but I know nothing about boats.'

'Yachts,' corrected Roy. 'You'll be fine old son', and he smiled for the first time.

Roy explained that we were to set sail in 12 hours' time and I gathered (he thought I knew) that we were to rendezvous with another boat in the middle of the Straits of Gibraltar. First, though, the other boat had to collect two tons of Moroccan Black from a beach somewhere. Some two-way radios that were meant to be delivered to us also didn't arrive. 'You sure your guv'nor's not ex-Army? He couldn't organise a piss-up in a brewery,' mumbled Roy as he dispatched me off in a car to fetch some. Six hours later I was back and a few hours later still the yacht sailed out of the marina.

For the first two days I was as sick as a dog and lay useless and bilious on the deck of the 40-foot yacht. Roy and even Bill just looked at me with scorn, wondering who this pratt was that had been foisted upon them. Three miles off the coast of Morocco we stopped and just bobbed up and down quietly as Roy tried to make radio contact with the other boat, I mean yacht. When it got dark, Roy lit the boat up like a Christmas tree. The radio crackled into life. 'We can see you. We can see you.'

'What is your position?' shouted Roy.

'We are about four miles down the coast from you.'

Off we chugged until we got level with a fleet of small rowing boats manned by small Moroccan men who immediately jumped to life and started hurling bale after bale of strong-smelling dope on to our decks. They were almost panicking in their hurry to get rid of their load and Roy was also anxious to get it on board. Bill and I scrabbled around, piling it up and securing the bales by rope underneath sheets of tarpaulin. When the loading was complete,

Roy opened up the throttle and we steamed back out into the Straits of Gibraltar. He saw a supertanker ahead and decided to tuck in behind it, where we would hopefully be hidden from any prying eyes. We were now due to rendezvous with another boat that would take the cargo on its onward journey. The next day a ferry boat cruised alongside us and we waved innocently to some holidaymakers. Anyone without a stinking cold could have guessed what our poorly secured and poorly hidden cargo was. The tarpaulin was like a mere sticking plaster on the top of an ugly black mound. It looked like the skies had opened and some higher being had opened its bowels and had a massive shit on our deck.

A guy called Crab was supposed to be in charge of the other craft and when, by our fifth day at sea, he hadn't turned up, Roy was ready to kill him. Roy was a tough man, not unlike the character Roy Shaw plays in the film *Jaws*, and had been the captain on a minesweeper during the Second World War. I had started to like him and feel safe in his capable hands. All our frustration, pain and anger was being focused on this fellow Crab. We were hungry, dehydrated, low on fuel and scared. Bill had cheered us up by informing us that in General Franco's Spain, drug smugglers received one year in prison for each kilo of puff they were caught with. I looked over at the 500-kilo mountain on the deck and felt sick. I thought of Howard fucking Marks sipping the finest wines and counting his money in his beautiful Italian retreat. Finally Roy cracked. 'Right, there's only one thing for it, we're going back into Cadiz.'

Bill and I were not sure about the wisdom of this but could see little alternative. We couldn't stay where we were, and sleep, food and liquid depravation were causing us problems in thinking straight. As we chugged into the harbour, I was appalled to see an unhealthy amount of people hanging around and clusters of people dining outside in harbour-side cafes. Roy spotted Crab and pulled up alongside him.

'Where the fuck have you been?' I screamed at this complete stranger as we pulled level.

'Our generator packed up, we've just got it fixed,' said Crab and then his eyes alighted on our very obvious cargo. 'Get the fuck out of here – there's police everywhere. Are you mad?'

Roy could see what he meant and tried to spin the vessel around, but in his haste the anchor chains from other boats somehow got caught up with something under ours and the waves from our sudden acceleration sent these boats crashing against the harbour wall. I winced as the sound of splitting wood and scraping metal prompted diners and other people around the harbour to stand up and crane their necks to see what the pandemonium was all about. Someone was bound to have told the harbour police as we pulled away from the flotsam and jetsam left by our escape but miraculously no official boat intercepted us. Besides carrying a harvest of hash we had seriously damaged at least three boats on our way out of the harbour. It was all I could do not to jump overboard, swim to the shore and take my chances. Somehow we all kept our nerve. Twelve miles out, Crab and his crew finally pulled alongside us. Roy, Bill and myself strained every muscle as we wasted no time slinging our load on to Crab's boat. The sweat was pouring off me and I just wanted the whole nightmare to end. I was expecting a police boat to arrive any second. Never again, I said, never again. Crab waved us goodbye and steered his boat apparently in the direction of Scotland. We headed back into Cadiz. I said goodbye to Roy and Bill and could not wait to return to the security and relative tranquility of Epsom.

Luckily my girlfriend Shirley remembered me, and the night after my return we went up to Leicester Square to see a film. I thought *Midnight Express* looked good. Trains have always captivated me. I loved *Casey Jones* on children's telly when I was a kid. To my horror, though, the movie told the true story of a young drug smuggler caught and subsequently imprisoned in a sadistic Turkish prison. Shirley was horrified by my reaction to the film. By the time we left the cinema I was trembling, sweating and tearful.

'What's the matter with you? That is the first time I've seen you show any feelings,' she asked.

'I just thought the film was quite realistic, that's all,' I replied defensively.

If I thought that my relationship with the 500 kilos of Moroccan Black was over, I was sadly mistaken.

'Do you remember that gear you loaded on to the boat?' drawled Howard a few days later down the telephone. I was hardly likely to forget it. 'Well, it has turned up in Scotland. I just wondered whether you could drive it down to London for us?'

'Actually, Howard, I'm a bit tied up,' I spluttered.

'It's worth thirty grand to you.' Howard knew by now how to motivate me. Suddenly I was untied. I had soon hired a car and was bounding up and down the motorway to collect 100 kilos at a time and deliver it to a meet somewhere in London. This was normally in open and busy places like Kensington High Street or the Kings Road, Chelsea, and I would simply open my boot and load the gear into the boot of the car of the man who had also double-parked in front of me. If a traffic warden or policeman chanced by we would say we were just delivering clothes to a shop and would not be a minute. From each run I would pinch a couple of kilos for private sale and I'm sure the men collecting from me did the same. Everyone had a dip each step of the way, right from the top down to the street dealer who'd weigh out a quarter or an eighth for a customer and nimbly break a lump off before wrapping it and passing it over. That was the nature of the beast and everyone knew and expected it.

Over the next 18 months, having won back Howard's confidence fully, he used me on a number of deals and I spent my time travelling first class around the world and staying in the best hotels. My work normally involved delivering and receiving cases of money, meeting people and putting the various strands of Howard's loose network in touch with each other. Rarely did I ever come into physical contact with any puff. There was no hierarchy or real structure in Howard's organisation but if he was the managing director then I like to think I was the operations manager. It constantly surprised and comforted me how nice and fundamentally decent most of the people that I had to deal with were. Howard Marks had been dubbed as Britain's most wanted criminal yet the people he dealt with came from diverse backgrounds and made up the most unlikely 'criminal' network ever. Inevitably I developed relationships with these people and started to think long and hard about doing deals off my own bat. With Howard I was paid good commission but I was still working for somebody else and that more than anything went against the grain.

In Epsom, one of my old schoolpals was now running a small business in the town. I had some cash that I needed to wash through an account and I asked him if he would pay £20,000 into his own personal account and then give me a cheque for only £18,000.

'Two grand for just paying a cheque into my account?' he said. 'It must be dodgy. Have you stolen it, Phil?'

'No, of course not. This is my savings from the street trading,' I lied. 'Paying you 10 per cent is better than giving the tax man 60 per cent.'

He thought about it and eventually agreed. I had put him in a difficult position because he only earned about £3,000 a year in his job.

'That was easy,' he beamed as he handed me over the cheque. 'Can we do it again?'

'Yes, I do have a bit more I could do with changing up.'

The following week I did another £15,000 with him. £35,000 was a huge amount of cash to be paying in to a small bank branch in leafy Surrey and I was not surprised to hear that my friend had received a letter from his bank a few days later closing his account and asking him to bank elsewhere. The problem was that elsewhere were not interested as he had been blacklisted. In fact, he recently told me it was only in the last couple of years that he has managed to re-enter the banking system. Sorry, mate.

Shirley and I had become serious by now. Roy had homed in on her first when he spotted her and a friend drinking in The Spread Eagle public house in Epsom. They had a brief relationship but, as always with Roy, his interest waned and slowly but surely Shirley and I became an item. She was very pretty, bubbly and ten years younger than me. By now she knew how I made my living. We shared a flat in a nice old house in Hammersmith and a guy called Francis had another flat in the house. Francis and I got on very well and we often passed the time of day. He never asked what I did for a living, which was a bit strange because it isn't usually long from when you meet someone that they do ask you that, and I never asked him. He was very knowledgeable and I thought he and Howard would get on well. When I finally introduced them, however, the blood drained from Howard's face. Later, when we were alone, he grabbed me.

'You've got to move out of here now,' he insisted. 'Your friend Francis is a drug smuggler.'

'Disgusting.'

Howard wasn't laughing. 'He's doing boatloads of Moroccan into the States. He's probably under surveillance by the Old Bill, Customs, the CIA, the FBI, the GPO, the PLO and anyone else you care to mention.'

It tickled me that Francis and I had been friends and were both careful to withhold from one another our profession, not having the faintest idea we were both smugglers. What were the odds on us independently renting rooms in the same house? I heard later that Francis was arrested as he sailed into New York with four tons of hash on board.

Shirley and I decided to pool our resources and buy a place. I had my Moroccan Black money and she'd been left a few quid by a relative so we bought a pleasant basement flat down in Brighton. I had always fancied living in Brighton: as a kid Mum and Dad had taken us down on day-trips and the place still stirred those childhood feelings of excitement in me. It used to be such a big day out, driving down there from Epsom or getting the train, but now with the new motorways it was less than an hour away. It didn't seem right.

My brother Tony had lived in Brighton and so had Howard. The gay community was just beginning to claim Brighton as their first English stronghold and they drank openly in The New Heart and Hand by the pier. Anywhere else at this time would have raised the wrath of the young local heterosexual males and they would have been attacked. There was still that *Brighton Rock* feel about the place, though. Not much but just enough. Smoky pubs with big mirrors remained from the Graham Greene era and, in summer, holidaymakers from London still bustled along between the piers and you could just about picture Pinkie and his boys weaving in and out of the throng.

Shirley became friendly with a gay chap called Andy. He was often around the flat and was almost part of the family. So much so that my business was often discussed in front of him. We both trusted him to be discreet. One evening Shirley and I were mulling over the latest proposition from a friend of Howard's. He had the knotty problem of 200 kilos of Thai grass sitting in a freight box at Heathrow Airport and he needed someone to go in there, sign for it and bring it out. Nobody knew whether the authorities were on to it and were merely waiting for it to be picked up, or if it was genuinely sitting there undiscovered. The chances of getting nicked were very high. I didn't fancy doing it and, to be fair, Howard's pal was not expecting me to, but he wondered if I knew anyone that would take the risk.

'I'm your man,' declared Andy.

'Don't be silly. You don't want to get involved in this sort of thing,' said Shirley. I'm sure Andy hadn't committed a criminal offence in his life. But Andy was insistent, even though I explained the downside to him as clearly as I could.

We arranged that Andy would hire a van and, armed with the relevant paperwork, would turn up at Heathrow and collect the freight box. I told him that as soon as the box was loaded he should get in the back and break into it, stick his hand in and feel inside for the Thai grass. If the grass was there, the chances were that we were all safe and he could drive back to Brighton and deposit it at the flat. However, if the grass was missing, then we had been sussed. Either way, Customs were not going to nick him there and then, as they would want to follow the onward trail and identify the Mr Big behind it all. Therefore, in the event that the grass was missing, I devised a route that Andy was to take. This would take him over Epsom Downs and past a small side road. In this side road would be waiting two likely lads from Epsom that I was paying to pull out as Andy passed and smash straight into the Customs car behind. It seemed simple but in my heart of hearts I knew the whole plan was fraught with risk. Therefore I also devised a plan C.

Sure enough, the grass was missing and the sweat must have poured from poor Andy's brow. He could see immediately that he was being followed by two cars with four men in each. As he came over the switchback on Epsom Downs he could see our car poised for the smash and flicked his lights to ensure they could see him coming. Andy kept his eye fixed on his mirror and although the back-up car edged forward, that was all it did. We learnt later the driver lost his bottle at the final second. These borstal boys were meant to be tough cases who had made a career out of TDA (Taking and Driving Away) but when it came to it they just couldn't do it. I should have known better. Andy kept his nerve and continued on with the contingency plan. He drove on to Maidstone College in Kent, pulled up outside the main entrance and leapt up the steps where, waiting just inside the entrance, were two more of my men. They flung a scarf around his neck, dropped a pile of textbooks into his arms and placed some horn-rimmed glasses on his face. Then the three of them came straight back out and ambled down the stairs chatting, passing eight determined-looking men leaping up the stairs. They didn't give Andy a second look: he looked more like *Dr Who* or *Lucky Jim* than a drugs courier.

Back at the flat we celebrated our daring escapade. OK, we had no grass but we had successfully evaded capture and detection in real style. The whole operation had been enormous fun but Andy looked troubled.

'What's up, Andy? You still get paid old son. Howard's friend is straight up like that.'

Andy continued to look down at the floor.

'Phil, you're going to do your nut. I've just realised something.'

'What's that, Andy?'

'I hired the van under my real name and address.'

The contents of my stomach dropped down to my lower bowel like a stone.

We hid Andy for a few days but heard both his own and his parents' houses had been busted. Police and Customs men were buzzing around Brighton like flies, determined to catch this little gang that had humiliated them so. A contact supplied a false passport and we persuaded Andy he had to leave the country for a few months (privately I knew it should be for a few years). He was dispatched to Bristol Airport from where he would fly to Zurich and interconnect with a flight to Bangkok. We had chosen Thailand for him to live for the foreseeable future. I thought he would like it.

At Zurich, a man who was also a well-known and highly recognisable TV actor would be in the transit lounge and would pass over a substantial amount of money in some hand luggage. The money was to help Andy establish himself in Thailand and to live on there but there was also a serious amount that had to be passed to someone else in Bangkok as a deposit on a future deal Howard and myself were involved with. Unfortunately, the actor, who liked a drink, had to wait in the transit lounge for quite a while and by the time Andy turned up he was lagging drunk. Andy knew who he was looking for because of the man's fame but the actor did not know who he was waiting for. In his drunken state he had asked several people if they were Andy. As Andy approached him, the man stood up but promptly lost his balance and fell into the table, smashing glasses and spilling ashtrays everywhere. Andy very briskly picked up his bag and left him to it.

The actor was put on a plane home back to London and came straight down to Brighton, possibly to see me, but was waylaid by a number of public houses on the way. He didn't leave them for months. I would see him around town as he descended into one of the longest drunken binges on record. He was living rough and the newspapers started to sniff around. I thought he would surely die but then all of a sudden he wasn't there. I was relieved to see him crop up on our television screens again soon after and it amused me when I'd catch him in a police programme as a police officer. The scripts always demanded that the police triumphed and the villains came a cropper, but I knew that he was as bent as a nine-bob note. However, I suppose it says a lot about the insecurity of his chosen profession when you can be a household name, or at least a household face, yet have no financial security. The term 'resting' in relation to actors and actresses is only funny to those outside the industry.

Back in Brighton the police had made the connection between Andy and Shirley. Inevitably they then progressed to me. Doors started coming down. Dad's door got kicked in, as did Shirley's parents' and my brother's. Shirley was arrested and held for a couple of days. They ended up believing her that she was a friend of Andy's but had not seen him for many weeks. But they were still keen to talk to me. I had no criminal record and was keen not to acquire one. Howard suggested I take myself off to Paris and lay low for a few weeks until the heat was off. This I did.

Shortly before this time I had obtained my first false passport. I assumed one of my old school pal's identities. It was easy enough: I knew his date and place of birth and his mother's maiden name. I had neglected to tell him about this or any of my activities; I never saw him those days anyway. Unfortunately the police did find out and assumed that he would know of my whereabouts and was in on the passport scam. They kicked his door down, pulled him in to Epsom police station and held him for two days waiting for him to crack. But, of course, he couldn't. He knew nothing and in the end the police realised it. Sorry again, mate.

Nearly a month later I returned to Brighton. As agreed, I had had no contact with anyone. When I reached the flat, my heart sank as I found it all locked up and through the window could see it was empty of furniture. Here we go again, I thought. Memories of the marital home in Walton-on-the-Hill that had been sold in my absence nearly a decade earlier jumped back into my mind. What is this effect I have on women?

I eventually tracked Shirley down to a health club, where she lay on a lounger draped in a white towel with a thick face-mask on. I looked her in the cucumbers and asked 'Shirley, what's going on?'

'I'm sorry, Phil, but I've found someone else.'

'Really? I didn't realise you were looking.'

'He's the manager of this club, actually.' She removed the cucumbers and pointed over to a smarmy-looking cunt standing in the doorway watching us.

'Fine. But I'm not just walking away empty-handed. I want my money out of the flat and I want the money out of the safe-deposit box.'

She argued that most of the money we put into the flat had been her inheritance and that the money in the safe-deposit box was compensation for what I had put her through. I didn't realise I had put her through anything. I know most girls don't expect to get banged up in the local nick or welcome having their parents' front door kicked in but this reaction seemed a bit extreme. She said she didn't want to spend the rest of her life with a criminal.

'You're the only fucking criminal around here,' I spat, 'you're robbing me blind.'

SQUATTING, FIBBING, EARNING – NORTHAMPTON AND BRIGHTON, ENGLAND

When I walked out of the health club, it dawned on me that my life had changed again radically. I was Shirleyless, homeless and potless. In 1973, I was wiped out financially by my wife but since then I had managed to put together a reasonable amount of money again. Here we were in 1980 and I was back in the same boat. This time, though, I was 30 years of age not a green teenager. I tried to call Howard and throw myself on his mercy but all his numbers had been changed. There was nothing sinister in this, it was something he did from time to time to keep the authorities off his trail. I had no idea where he was. He could have been anywhere in the world.

Disorientated, I walked from the health club to Brighton railway station. I had £6 in my pocket. My last £6. I took a train to Victoria with the vague idea of heading down to Dad's but realised the police would still be looking for me there. Instead I got on the tube and alighted at Euston station. Looking up at the board I saw that the first train out was going to Northampton. I was obviously not thinking rationally because I boarded it. I loved Shirley and I was really hurting. The shock of losing her so coldly consumed me. I was hurting like I had never hurt before. As time went by, the shock of losing my money again would hurt even more.

At Northampton I walked out of the station and turned left. It was a bitterly cold night. I had no idea where I was going. I was down to a couple of quid in my pocket. As I passed a near-derelict house I could see the glow of a fire inside. The door was ajar and I walked into the room where I had seen the glow. The fire was burning, not in the fireplace, but in the centre of the room, and sitting around it were three men and a girl. They were passing a joint between them and a cassette player in the corner of the room was playing Steel Pulse.

'Hi, would you mind if I got warm for a bit?'

'Sure,' said one of the men. It was obviously not that unusual for people to come off the street and walk into this house. One of the men was convinced I had visited before. They asked if I had any gear but I told them no and that actually I had only £2 to my name. I think that was when I went up in their estimation.

'Welcome to the squat, man.'

I spent Christmas with this motley but likeable bunch of squatters. The line-up changed almost weekly. Some of them were plastic squatters and came just for the day from their mum and dad's nice semi-detached houses in town. Like day boys at a boarding school. The purpose of the squat seemed to be the procurement, sale and consumption of marijuana. The fact that I didn't partake amazed them and was partly responsible, I think, for them accepting me so quickly. I would not be a drain on their main resource. It amazed me how their lives were focused around smoking. They discussed the qualities of the puff in detail and time and time again.

'Red Leb is much better than Black.'

'You're joking, man. You can't beat Moroccan Black.'

'Yes you can, Thai sticks, man. Blow your fucking head off.'

Then hours and hours seemed to be spent preparing the stuff for smoking in home-made contraptions made from Fairy Liquid bottles and pipe bowls. They called them bongs. After the 'blow' had been inhaled, they'd fall into deep conversations about the music they were playing. A song called 'Hurricane' by Bob Dylan seemed to fascinate them and they would have the same discourse about this wrongly convicted black American boxer over and over again. I was familiar with people talking bollocks to one another after taking amphetamines. The general feeling of well-being causes people to gush for hours about nothing in particular. There are few worse punishments than having to spend an evening with someone who has taken a handful of speed tablets when you yourself are straight. I had enough nights like this in Epsom when bombers, purple hearts and French blues were all the rage in the late 1960s and early 1970s. These squatters were talking similar bollocks but it was slower, more introspective and, because their eyelids became extremely heavy and often closed, they did not realise you weren't listening.

I wondered if they had smoked any of the Moroccan Black I had wrestled with in the Straits of Gibraltar and later transported down from Scotland. There was a pretty good chance they would have but I felt it prudent to keep my past to myself. I told them that my girlfriend had finished with me and I'd had a sort of nervous breakdown. Perhaps this was true.

John Lennon was murdered while I was staying there and this caused the squatters great distress. Marijuana was puffed with more urgency. A couple of the guys got all weepy. Tapes of Lennon's latest album *Double Fantasy* arrived, as did back collections of Beatles music. At least we had moved on from 'Hurricane'. Lennon's death made me think of Howard in his New York prime. I think Howard was based for a time near the Dakota Mansions where the former Beatle was gunned down and he often talked about him. I don't know if they met or not but if they hadn't, it wouldn't have been for want of Howard trying.

Thinking of Howard and Lennon sort of galvanised me into action. I began rising early in the morning and stealing milk from the doorsteps of our not so near neighbours. This was the least I could do to pay for my keep. A few weeks ago I'd been flying around the world first class and now I was furtively pinching milk bottles from doorsteps in the early hours of the morning. During the day I earned loose change around the Northampton pubs by performing little card tricks I'd learnt from the punters in Dad's bookies when I was a kid. This was enough to buy me coffee and rolls in the coffee bar in Northampton Station. The rest of the coins went into a public payphone, from where I started to call around all the contacts I could think of who might be able to give me a helping hand. Most of them spurned me, others I could not get hold of and I had to leave messages. Each day I had to spend most of the time at my new 'office' in case someone phoned back.

Eventually in late January 1981, after ten weeks as a squatter, someone did phone me back. Through Howard I had met a few pop stars. He made a habit of befriending them and it wasn't unknown for him to wash his money through the financing of obscure albums, recording studios and the like. There is no easier way to lose money. See, Howard wanted fame more than anything. Even more than money. His ideal occupation would have been a rock star but when even he had to accept this was not going to happen, he did the next best thing and got involved with the managing side. P.J. Proby had been one of his early causes, though he was completely unaware of the source of Howard's income. Howard was always trying to orchestrate his comeback. I was never quite sure what he was coming back from. Sometimes I got roped into getting him to a gig but got fed up with trying to get him out of the pub. Mind you, I could understand what Howard saw in him. When you did get Jim on stage, and his mood was right, he could, as they say, tear the place apart, as well as his trousers.

Howard had an endearing habit of investing my money for me. Sometimes when he was due to pay me he would say 'I've taken £15,000 to invest in this or invest in that.' I normally went along with him as these money-washing diversions were often great fun. One such diversion was the formation of ZAP Productions. I was the P, Howard was the A (for Albi, one of his aliases) and the Z was another investor. Our first investment was the financing of a documentary about, wait for it, P.J. Proby. We sent him up to a big rented Elizabethan House in Berkhamstead and proceeded to surround him with a full film crew. If I remember correctly, the film was called *Life After Elvis*. Proby was probably one of the first Elvis impersonators; he was at it when the King was still alive. It all came to nothing as far as we were concerned and nobody bought the film. However, Howard had successfully raised Proby's profile because, soon after, he landed the part of Elvis in a West End show.

It wasn't Proby who unwittingly came to my rescue in Northampton, it was Bean. He had been the frontman of a successful 1960s pop group who had enjoyed a top-five hit. He remained a household name and his solitary hit is an all-time classic but further pop chart success eluded him. However he had made some money and kept himself busy with session work and preparing his comeback. I told him about my own express ride into oblivion and he very kindly agreed to loan me £500. He had no idea what my line of business was. Bye bye squat. Bye bye Northampton.

I used the £500 to get myself a false passport; although my head was back together, I was still officially on the run and I was not going to risk giving myself up. I thought the police would have trouble getting me on the Heathrow freight box rap as I had had nothing to do with its importation but I fancied that they may have by now linked me to Howard and other people they were no doubt aware of. Therefore, in February 1981, I left Philip Sparrowhawk behind in a Northampton squat with the roaches and the bongs and walked out into the fresh air as Brian Meehan, Irish national with an Irish passport. It was a strange but liberating moment.

I booked a flight to Vancouver, Canada, where a couple of friends were now living. One of them had been one of the few people to call my Northampton station concourse office back when my luck was down. They weren't doing any business but introduced me to some contacts who were keen to get a load of Thai grass into the country. Demand was high in Canada but supply limited. I bullshitted them that I was on top of my game and the head of a cannabis smuggling network and they went for it. My friends had laid some groundwork and I am sure would have dropped a few names around me, including Howard's. We negotiated a price of C$400,000 for four tons of quality Thai sticks. The Canadian buyers were absolute gentlemen: they put me up in the best hotel and treated me generally like a VIP. They were so trusting they advanced me C$50,000 on the deal. I had the cash under my bed and as I lay awake in a Vancouver hotel room I marvelled at the twists and turns a life could take. Less than 100 hours earlier I had been living in a squat and shitting in a toilet with no flush, with no money to my name. Now I had C$50,000 in a briefcase under my bed. What I didn't have, though, was any of the Thai sticks that I had promised to deliver.

I called Todd in Bangkok. I had first met Todd when I passed some money over to him in the Dusit Thani Hotel in Bangkok on one of my first errands for Howard. I didn't beat around the bush and told him I had a big deal going down with the Canadians and was giving him the opportunity to participate.

'They are prepared to pay C$300,000,' I told him.

'That sounds good to me,' Todd replied. Good for me as well. I was now C$100,000 in front on this deal already. Todd invited me down to Los Angeles to his parents' house for a few days, to tie up the details and have a little break. To do this I had to visit the US Embassy in Vancouver and obtain a visa. The man on the desk looked at my false Irish passport and said, 'Mr Meehan, do you have any relatives in America?'

'Yes, about 16,000.'

He laughed, stamped my passport and handed it back to me.

At Los Angeles airport I booked into a small hotel nearby. Todd had not yet arrived from Bangkok and I didn't fancy turning up at his parents' place before him. At the reception the young lady looked at my passport and beamed at me. 'You're Irish. I bet you're a happy man today.'

Not having the faintest idea what she was on about, I smiled politely and went to my room. Perhaps Ireland had won a football match or something. Unlikely, but possible. Americans can be strange. An hour later I was relaxing on the bed when the phone rang.

'Mr Meehan, hi there, I'm Steve, the manager of this motel here. I wondered if you would like to join me in the bar for a little drink?'

'I'm a bit tired from my flight, Steve. Thanks anyway. Maybe I'll pop down a bit later.'

'Sure thing, Mr Meehan, we'll be waiting for you.'

I know that Americans have a proactive approach to hospitality but the call unsettled me a little. Surely the manager does not call every single guest and invite him or her to the bar for a drink? Unless he's a lonely alcoholic. I settled back and enjoyed the novelty of a television with hundreds of channels. Back in England we only had three; in Northampton we didn't even have a television. An hour later the phone rang again and there was a chirpy female voice at the other end; I think it was the girl who had booked me in, chattering away.

'Mr Meehan, Steve and the rest of the staff and some of the guests are all in the bar; it would really be an honour if you could join us for a drink. We're having a real great time down here.'

'OK,' I sighed, trying and failing to sound a bit enthusiastic, 'I'll be down in a few minutes.'

An honour? Who do they think I am? They must think I am some sort of celebrity, I decided, but I could not think of anyone with the name Brian Meehan. There was a Tony Meehan who played with The Shadows but that was 20 years ago and I don't think The Shads were big in America. I tucked my shirt into my trousers, slipped my shoes on and walked down into the bar.

The whole place was decked out in green. Irish tricolors hung from the ceiling, the staff were wearing green blazers and Irish tiddly music was blaring out of the speakers. To my horror a home-made banner was draped across the bar – WELCOME BRIAN MEEHAN.

'Mr Meehan, can I call you Brian?' This must be Steve, the manager. 'Thanks for coming down, Brian. We're having our St Patrick's Day bash and when you booked in, a real-life Irishman, well, we thought we'd make it in your honour.'

At this point the receptionist came over and handed me over a pint of something green. On the run from the police, setting up a large drug deal, this could only happen to me.

'Do you know the O' Neills from Waterford?' By now there was a small crowd around me.

'My family came from Galway Bay, whereabouts from the home country do you live, Brian?'

I had never been to Ireland in my life and knew little about the geography of the place. I deflected this question by saying I had lived in London for some years.

'It's criminal what the English bastards are doing to Bobby, don't you think Brian?' Bobby? Bobby who? Bobby Moore? Bobbie Gentry? This was getting a bit hairy and if I wasn't careful my non-Irishness would be exposed. Thankfully the man who asked me this last question thrust a folded newspaper under my nose. Bobby Sands, an IRA prisoner and hunger striker, was contesting a by-election from his prison cell.

'Criminal,' I agreed, and shook my head in disgust at the English bastards.

In the best *News of The World* fashion, I soon made my excuses and headed for the safety of my room, leaving this room full of Irish militants, most of whom had never visited the country in their lives either, to serenade and pine for their homeland together. When Todd turned up and I told him about the evening's events, he laughed hysterically and said it sounded like a bad acid trip.

Todd and I flew back to Thailand together. I based myself at gay Andy's flat. I was probably the last person he wanted to come back into his life and also my presence cramped his style. As I had predicted, Andy liked Thailand. In fact, he loved Thailand. He had a reasonable lifestyle and had quickly learnt the Thai language and adapted well to the way of life. He found their relaxed attitudes to sexual orientation particularly enlightening.

Todd made arrangements with his people up in the north of

Thailand and he took me up there to an army base where the goods would be packed up and crated. I was satisfied that the wheels were in motion. I called the Canadians and told them delivery would be in ten weeks. They were delighted with this and at their own behest they flew into Thailand and handed me over another C$150,000. The balance would be paid on safe arrival in Canada. I gave Todd C$100,000 and told him his final CS$200,000 would be paid on arrival. I now had C$100,000 to my name, give or take a thousand, and had little else to do on this one. Brian Meehan was in business. It must have been the quickest and easiest one-tenth of a million ever made at the time. I had been contemplating fighting Shirley for a share of our money but now this seemed inconsequential.

Suddenly, however, it appeared that Brian Meehan's luck was as volatile as that of Philip Sparrowhawk's. Andy came back to the flat one morning and when I picked up the *Bangkok Post* that he had brought back with him I was horrified to see Todd's picture on the front page below a headline screaming BUSTED! Somehow he had been apprehended driving the lorries out of the northern army base. I found out later that he had tried to avoid or reduce the bribes he should have been paying to the people that mattered at the base. This was rank stupidity. There's breaking the rules and breaking the rules. I couldn't jump up and go and see Todd straight away, as this would bring suspicion on me, so I spent a fraught few days twiddling my thumbs and wondering what the hell I was going to do. Finally the Canadians called and I knew I had to face them. Maybe they had heard about Todd.

'There's been a bit of a problem this end,' I lied. 'There's been a delay but you'll have your goods within two weeks.' Why do I say things like that?

'Brian, there's been a problem this end too,' the Canadian said. 'We've had a shipment in from Pakistan and it's been busted. Shit's flying. Can you hold fire at your end? We'll be back in touch when the heat dies down. Sorry about this Brian, does this cause you a serious problem?'

I could have kissed the man. He hadn't mentioned the C$200,000 I had already received.

'It shouldn't be a problem, but it will cost to keep it in storage. People want paying well for holding that sort of amount.'

'Of course, Brian, we fully understand that. Take the storage fees from the deposit. Is that OK?'

'That's fine.'

With the pressure off, I went to see Todd in prison. He couldn't have been more apologetic. I decided not to tell him that the heat was off and pretended that I was angrier than I really was. To his credit, despite his own predicament he arranged for me to get hold of another four tons and gave me the number of a Thai solicitor with the unlikely name of Neil. The solicitor later informed me that Neil was a Thai name before it was ever adopted in England. Before I went to visit Neil in Bangkok, though, I heard from the Canadians again. My luck could not get better.

'Brian, look, we're really sorry but we will have to postpone the deal indefinitely. Things are coming on top for some of us and we really cannot risk a further shipment. Now, we understand this is highly irregular. We're embarrassed about the whole thing and are sorry you won't be able to collect all of your fee. Hopefully the money you've had has covered your expenses and inconvenience and you will work with us again sometime.'

Fucking hell! I was now C$100,000 in front with no obligation to the Canadians, and Todd had put me on to another deal for four tons where the source had been paid their deposit and I was set to collect the rest of whatever price I got, less another C$200,000 to the source when I finally sold the consignment.

Neil put me on to Barry, an Australian now living in Pattaya in Thailand, who he said would have some ideas on where to send the four tons. Barry had been a professional shoplifter in Australia but had retired to a life on the beach with his new Thai wife. Barry's father was Jack 'the Fibber' Warren, another shoplifter, bank and diamond thief and an extremely well-known criminal in his home country.

Pattaya had been a picturesque fishing village only some 20 years earlier but had started to be patronised by American GIs from a nearby military base. During the Vietnam War, American sailors joined the soldiers. Soldiers and sailors attract prostitutes. Prostitutes attract tourists. Tourists attract restaurants and hotels. By the 1970s, Pattaya had taken off. There were prostitutes aplenty in Bangkok but the sex trade was not the focus of the place as it was in Pattaya. In every roadside bar they sat on stools in chattering groups of five or six in their tight dresses and attempted to tempt Westerners to sample their delights. When the Brits started arriving, they didn't have to try too hard. You could see the attraction for English men. They were young, pretty, cheap and, most importantly, seemed to enjoy their work. In Britain, experiences with prostitutes could be seedy affairs where the client was forbidden to show affection and the meter was always running. Prostitutes on the street, at least, were often fearsome-looking creatures, long past their sell-by date with big hair and badly applied lipstick. Thai girls were keen to please. They liked to wash their client, pander to his every need and whim and stay with him for the whole night or longer. Of course, some of them wanted the client to fall for them and then they would have a chance of a passport, but most people got the same treatment. It is a Thai characteristic to enjoy their work and to laugh and generally be happy and it is one of their most endearing traits. It is not uncommon to see Thai workers in the backbreaking toils of the paddy field laughing and joking with one another. Prostitution was no different. This is why Englishmen sometimes fool themselves into believing these girls are not on the game and that they are their genuine girlfriends. This is why some continue to send them or their families money when they have returned to England, in the naive belief that the girl is waiting faithfully for their return.

It also has to be remembered that prostitution has no serious stigma in Thailand. It is a mainly poor country where there are few avenues of work open to girls. A girl from a country village who had been to Pattaya or Bangkok to work would be accorded a special respect when she returned home a few years later, wiser and slightly richer. You don't see prostitutes over 30 years of age in Pattaya.

That first time I went down to find Barry I was shocked by the tits-in-your-face character of Pattaya. 'You want massage? Love you long time,' wailed the girls as I walked along the Pattaya Bay road. Some grabbed me by the arm squealing 'Fuckee fuckee,' and tried to run away with me as I jumped off the back of my tuk-tuk. They had to get you while you were fresh. The reaction a new white face triggered was like a busy Istanbul bazaar where the traders crowd you trying to persuade you to come into *their* shop and buy a carpet. The difference was that the goods on offer here were olive brown flesh not Persian rugs.

Barry took me into the bars where the lady-boys, called *katoeys*, draped themselves around the walls, also awaiting clients. These were homosexual boys and men who had taken transvestitism to its limits. You could tell them apart from the girls because they were taller and had stronger jaws. If you looked closely, they had prominent Adam's apples. But if you were new, not forewarned, or just drunk, you could easily be fooled. Some of them were exceptionally beautiful. Plenty were fooled. Plenty didn't need to be fooled. Men with wives and kids back home came here especially for the lady-boys. There were two lads from London in the bar that first night and they were lapping up the atmosphere. This was beyond their understanding. Back home they were just coming to terms with closet doors opening and all manner of people jumping out. Their natural reaction on meeting a homosexual would be to abuse or even assault them. Here they were in a bar full of them but instead of feeling disgust their loins were twitching. This was not meant to happen. They couldn't admit it to one another. One lady-boy glided across the bar and rested his head delicately on one of the Londoner's shoulders. He stepped to one side but he was studying the complexion, and the breasts.

'You're beautiful, you are.' This just slipped out – he was

transfixed – but when he realised what he had said, he hurriedly added 'mate'. These days the lines are even more blurred with the lady-boys as they save up their Baht and have operations to remove their Adam's apples and have their genitals reconstructed as vaginas.

Barry arranged for the four tons to get into Australia packed in with a shoe consignment. It went like a dream and I was soon flying on to Oz to pick up A\$2 million. After doing so, I took Barry up on his suggestion that I drop in on his father, Jack the Fibber, while I was in the country. Jack was a fearsome man and to describe him as a mere shoplifter was stretching the belief muscle a bit. It soon became apparent that Jack was sitting quite high up the Australian crime tree. As such he was the first gangster I had any dealings with. While I was with him, I saw him in action. He had stolen a very expensive diamond-encrusted ring in a robbery and was taking it to a fence to sell. The fence said he would give Jack A\$40,000 for it so God knows what it was worth on the open market. Jack agreed but he switched the ring for one that looked identical, one he had had made earlier for the very purpose of conning the fence. Back at his house some days later the fence rang. I could hear him shouting down the phone at Jack.

'You bastard, Jack. You've had me over. The ring you sold me is a dud, Jack, I want my money back or I want the real ring. This is not a game, Jack. I can have you killed just like that. And I will, Jack. Do you hear?'

Jack was putting the phone to my ear so I could hear. He thought it was one big joke and just hung up on the bloke.

'Are you not worried, Jack?'

'He's fuck all. He can't have me killed. I'll tear his fucking head off. Come on, follow me and we'll have some fun.'

I did, but with some trepidation that there might be violence involved. When we got to the fence's house, however, Jack was charm personified.

'Look, I'm sorry, but I've been conned too. Someone has switched on me. You know I wouldn't do that to you. I'm sad you can think that. How long have we been doing business together? I'm going to get the ring back for you but, look, I have no real cash. Can you lend me $5,000 so I can open the door with this fella? You'll have your ring by tomorrow.'

'There you are,' laughed Jack as we drove back to his place, 'a lesson in how to squeeze another $5,000 out of someone you've just conned out of $40,000.'

Although he was an incorrigible crook, Jack treated me well and was great company. I parked outside his place with the A$2 million in the boot of my hired car and joined him and some cohorts for drinks. He told me his first arrest had been in 1938 for riding on the footboard of a tram and then he had become a shoplifter. He was particularly proud of being part of the Kangaroo Gang that had travelled from Australia to the UK and Europe and carried out some daring raids on high-class jewellers using beautiful women as decoys. Whilst we sat in his house reminiscing about his legendary exploits and laughing in all the right places, the door burst open and dozens of Melbourne's finest stormed in. There was a warrant for 60-year-old Jack's arrest. In the mêlée I just managed to slip away and drive my A$2 million and me as far away as possible.

Jack had put me on to someone who, for 10 per cent of my Aussie dollars, would transfer the money to a safe bank in Hong Kong. How bad was that? Back in Thailand I was a seriously wealthy man. Six months earlier I had been traipsing around Brighton dazed and with six quid in my pocket. I decided to take a breather. I needed it. Especially when I heard that Todd got 15 years. That concentrated the mind a little. I would use my money to do what I could to arrange his release or perhaps escape.

I bought myself a nice pad in Bangkok and left Andy to his own devices. We were both relieved. I fell more and more in love with Thailand. I started to soak up the history and the culture and enrolled in a language school. The only thing I had known about Thailand before I got there was that it used to be called Siam and Yul

Brynner and Deborah Kerr starred in a film called *The King and I* that was supposedly based on the Thai royal family. I don't know if it's any good as I've never seen it, but the Thais have and they hate it. You've got more chance of seeing a Jackie Mason show in Baghdad than catching *The King and I* on television or in the cinema in Thailand. They say they have never been colonised by a foreign power, although during the Second World War they sided with the Japanese, who entered Thailand. When the bomb dropped on Hiroshima, however, the Thais quickly changed allegiances. The Thais are a pragmatic people. Beneath the happy-go-lucky smiling exterior exists a tough race and neighbours or foreign powers cross the Thais at their peril. I learnt that the worst thing for Thais is to lose face, whether as individuals or as a nation. They do not like physical confrontation. If you are in a car accident in Bangkok (and if you are driving in Bangkok the chances are you will be), it does not pay to scream and shout. This is worse than assaulting someone. You might end up having a bullet put through your head and if you do then someone will be along taking photographs for the *True Life Murder* picture magazine.

At the language school I met a young 16-year-old girl called Pao. She was learning English and we agreed to continue to teach each other our native languages after classes. We fell in love and decided to set up home together. Her family, who were good country folk from the mountainous area of northern Thailand, were furious. Sadly they would not speak to Pao for two years. If they had known then what they do now I could understand this but, as far as they were all concerned, I was the Far East marketing manager for a soap powder company. Don't ask me where that came from – by then lies tumbled from my mouth like confetti. Many Thai families would have considered it a result for their daughter. Most country girls if they left home ended up working abroad in domestic service or prostitution. I couldn't have been that bad a proposition. Could I?

BARRY, SYDNEY AND THE PINEAPPLE CHUNKS – SYDNEY, AUSTRALIA

A few months later I decided to travel south down to Pattaya to revisit Barry. I was not looking to do more business. I liked him, enjoyed his company and was going to bung him a few quid if he needed it. Barry would never know how well I had done out of the Australia drop. Staying with him those few days I noticed he had a heroin habit. It wasn't hard to figure out: if you're young and inject yourself regularly it is either diabetes or heroin. He seemed in control of it but nevertheless it saddened me. Inevitably our conversations got around to dope and Barry said he thought there was an opportunity to move Indian hash into Australia. Jack the Fibber and his friends had Sydney Airport tied up. If we could get a shipment out of India it would definitely clear Sydney Airport – and Jack was not fibbing. I offered to fly to Bombay to check it out. I went first class and was the only one in that section of the plane. I was just making myself comfortable when a hostess approached me.

'There is a lady at the back who is not feeling too well. Would you object if she sat up here with you where we can keep an eye on her?'

Thinking there could be an outside chance of joining the mile-high club, I readily agreed. Any notions along those lines were soon banished when the hostesses helped a frail old lady into the seat next to me. She was hunched over and dressed in a pale blue gown. Her face was framed in nun-type headgear, the pattern and colour of which made me look twice because for a fleeting second I thought she was wearing my dad's favourite tea-towel from home.

'This is Mother Teresa,' the hostess informed me. We shook hands and soon fell into conversation. Her English was good and she was very knowledgeable about my home country – Ireland. She assumed I was Catholic. She told me she was Albanian but had been working with the poor and sick in Calcutta for many years. I found her company exhilarating: she was sharp with a great sense of humour and not at all over-pious. She told me about her work and the suffering endured in parts of India. Not once did she ask what I did. I'm glad she didn't because her presence was so profound I think I might have confessed all to her there and then. Instead I pulled out $10,000 and asked if she would accept it as a donation to her charity. She was only mildly shocked and looked at me sympathetically, as though she knew I was attempting to assuage my guilt. When we got off the plane, I carried her luggage and, as we went into the airport terminal, photographers were snapping and reporters jostling each other to get a few words. The next day Phil Sparrowhawk, masquerading as Brian Meehan and arriving in Bombay to set up a drugs deal, was plastered all over the papers coming through the airport with Mother Teresa. When we parted, she wished me luck and urged me to visit her mission. I had an altogether different mission to fulfil.

My contact in Bombay was a chap named Bill. He said he could get me 500 kilos of Kashmir hash. That sort of weight would be valued at around £2.5 million and a quick calculation told me that if all went well I would personally cream off a million pounds from this deal. This was major, major league. I sampled the goods visually and burnt some and sniffed. Seemed good to me. When Bill asked for some cash expenses, I told him he'd have to wait until the following day because I had given $10,000 to a charity on the plane. He looked at me as if I was mad.

'You'll be working for Mother Teresa next,' he laughed.

I even stayed around to watch Bill's people get the cargo on the plane. He had arranged for the hash to be stacked in with a consignment of bathroom tiles. Six hours after the plane had taken off I took a call from Barry.

'You'll never believe this, Phil, the commie bastards at Sydney have gone on strike. It's the first time ever. The cunts have just walked out and our plane has been diverted to Melbourne.'

Barry went on to tell me that his father had some contacts in Melbourne but they were not as strong. Some bent airport workers at that end had agreed to clear our goods but they wanted 50 per cent of them.

'That's a bit steep, Barry,' I ventured.

'We don't really have a choice, Phil, do we.' Barry was telling not asking.

The consignment got through and I ended up drawing £300,000 – a nice amount but only a third of what I had been building myself up for.

When I was working for Howard, I was basically on commission. Now, by sourcing the product myself, I had transformed my finances beyond belief. I had gone from courier, to retailer, to wholesaler. The next logical step would have been to become the manufacturer. I travelled Thailand talking to farmers and striking deals to buy their crop. I might agree to buy a ton of grass for A$12,000. I would then need to pay around A$4,000 for transport of the product and then another A$1,000 for its storage awaiting transportation. Add to this another A$2,000 to local girls for cleaning the crop (Thai sticks need to look like Thai sticks, for example) and a further A$15,000 for packaging. This was expensive because the packing could be complex. I remember one time, for example, when a consignment was packed into various fairground figures made in Thailand but bound for Australian theme parks. These included life-size Mickey Mouse figures and horses with poles through their backs. That consignment got through a bit too quickly as some moved on in their journey across Australia before their cargo could be unpacked. Therefore, somewhere in Australia, Mickey Mouse is carrying. On top of all this there would be the A$5,000 for the legitimate shipping and a final A$20,000 bribe to the appropriate customs officials to see the load through. This was a total outlay of some A$70,000, but, of course, I would insist on A$150,000 up front from the customer so there was no actual risk of me losing out. The ton of Thai sticks would fetch A$4 million on the streets of Australia and I would expect a commission of 10 per cent. Therefore, my total take on a one-ton Aussie deal would be A$550,000, about £300,000.

The commission would normally be paid. Your customer wanted to ensure that you got the product through OK. If you were banking on the commission, you'd make sure you did your best to get it through. Also, the customer would want to use you again and if they defaulted on the commission they knew that would not be likely.

As you can imagine, it did not take many such deals operating from the top of the chain to accumulate serious wealth. Whatever way I looked at it I was now a millionaire. It had been an ambition of mine to make my first million by the time I was 20 years of age. That didn't happen. I didn't quite manage it by 30 either but here I was at 33 with, for me, unimaginable wealth. They say money comes to money and it is true. Money buys opportunity. It enables you to be in the right place at the right time. You do the same sort of deals but they simply have more noughts on the end. Not having to worry about losing some affords you the luxury of being able to punt. If a deal or venture goes wrong – so what? The next one or the one after that will work.

Things back in England were looking up. The last few years had been a miserable time politically and economically, or so it seemed. Towards the end of the 1970s the Labour Government had been looking tired and the trade unions appeared to be walking all over everyone. The Prime Minister was a bloke called James Callaghan but he was a forgotten man even before he left office, such was his charisma and impact. British Leyland were making cars that nobody wanted to buy, the dustmen went on strike and city centres were piled high with mounds of festering rubbish. Entrepreneurs were being punished through the tax system for attempting to create wealth and Shakin' Stevens kept bringing out records. The ultimate ignominy was when our chancellor Denis Healey was forced to go to the International Monetary Fund with his begging bowl. Hello old chap, welcome to the Third World.

In 1979 Mrs Thatcher became Prime Minister and my first reaction was one of despair. She looked and spoke like the stuck-up headmistress of a Worthing prep school. All stiff shoulders, hairspray and clunky brooches. I didn't fancy Britain being run by a Women's Institute Government. We might bake better cakes for the church fête but what about the state of the nation? Like most people I was wrong about her. She made decisions: some of them may have been wrong, but at least she made them. Things started to happen. The national debt was decreased. Taxes became more equitable. She even got money back from those wastrels in the Common Market. People got off their arses. It was what we needed at the right time. By the time I invited Barry up to stay with me in Bangkok and celebrate our Melbourne airport success, she had invaded the Falkland Islands and reclaimed them from Argentina who had reclaimed them from us. I remember listening to the developments on the BBC World Service and noticing how the public-school-voiced announcers, who prided themselves on their absolute neutrality, could not disguise their triumphalism. It did occur to me that Britain owning these islands was akin to Argentina occupying the Isle of Wight but I soon dismissed the thought. It felt good. You can take the man out of England but you cannot take England out of the man.

One fateful day Barry and I went drinking at lunchtime. I was not going to share his poison so he agreed to share mine. By nine o' clock in the evening, after visiting dozens of Bangkok's finest bars, I retired home as drunk as a skunk. Barry had the taste and perhaps he was going to have a lady, so he stayed out. I can remember him coming in after midnight. He was obviously legless because his banging around and ascent of the stairs woke me. In the morning I felt reasonably fresh but decided not to wake Barry because I figured he'd be dead to the world. I went around to Andy's and together we went out for breakfast. After picking up a few items of shopping I jumped in a cab back to the house. As I paid the driver, Pao and the maid came running down the path to me, screaming and crying.

'Barry's dead.'

'Barry, he dead.'

I ran into the house thinking he probably wasn't. He might be in an alcohol or heroin-induced coma. But when I went into his room he *was* dead to the world. I touched his forehead and he was so cold. Unnaturally cold. The cold of a dead body is like nothing else. He must have been dead for hours. There was no point in trying to resuscitate him and there was no point in phoning an ambulance. Instead I called the police. 'Someone has died in my house,' I said, and gave them the address. Pao and the maid were inconsolable. The poor maid had taken him in a cup of coffee and discovered his body.

The police arrived and I wished I'd explained myself better. They screeched into the road in a convoy with sirens blaring. Armed police took crouching positions and I raised my hands in the air. One came up and pressed a pistol into the flesh of my neck. They love *The Streets of San Francisco* in Thailand. I detailed to them as best I could what had happened and, looking around at the state of Pao and the maid, they relaxed a bit. I would even go as far as to say that they were disappointed. A doctor examined Barry and announced that he had suffered a drug overdose. Fortunately I had emptied Barry's pockets and belongings of all his drug paraphernalia before the entire Bangkok police force descended upon us, but the mention of drugs got them excited again.

'He is a friend,' I insisted, 'but I had no idea he was a drug user. We went out last night. I came in at nine and he stayed out. I heard him come in and go to bed at about twelve. He was drunk when I left him and he was drunker when he came in. He took no drugs in my presence.'

This was almost true. The police seemed satisfied and departed almost as fast as they had come, leaving Barry still upstairs on the bed. We made ourselves coffee. Two ambulance men then arrived and I took them up to Barry. He was a big man, like his father, and Thais are generally very small. They struggled to get Barry's body out on to the landing. Not only was he very heavy but rigor mortis was setting in. I went back downstairs but to my absolute horror, when I heard some thudding and went to investigate, I saw they had taken a leg each and were dragging Barry down the stairs behind them. His head was thudding on each step as they yanked his poor corpse downward.

'Stop! Stop!' I yelled, jumping behind Barry and cradling his head. The image of poor Barry and the undignified end to his life still will not leave me. I would like it to.

'Where are you taking him?' I asked.

'Police want autopsy.'

'That's fucking great. It'll look like I bashed his brains in now.' The ambulancemen gently bowed, smiled and drove Barry away.

That afternoon we had to make a number of difficult phone calls. I spoke to Barry's family in Australia, although Jack was not around. I was dreading telling him myself. Pao broke the news in Pattaya. The rest of the afternoon and evening we sat and reminisced about him. He was a great laugh. Pao reminded me of how when she first met Barry on our first trip to Australia, her grasp of the English language was still rudimentary. He had told her that it was the custom in his country that when paying shop assistants or tipping waiters to say 'Gitfucked'. She obediently did this until I had to put a stop to it in case someone smacked her in the mouth.

That night Pao and I heard noises downstairs and I got up to investigate. It was the police and they were unplugging my TV and stereo and carrying them down the path to a waiting police car.

'What are you doing?' The man who had held the gun at my throat earlier pulled out his gun again. He did not speak. He didn't have to. His colleagues continued to pillage anything portable that was worth taking. Then they left. I knew all about police corruption, it was institutionalised here, but this was ridiculous. A light had come on in my next-door neighbour's house and I went around to see him. He was a well-to-do man who worked for the Thai Farmer's Bank.

'I've just been burgled.' I was still astounded.

'Call the police.'

'It was the police.'

My neighbour stared at me. He would surely have heard about Barry's body being loaded into the ambulance the previous afternoon.

'You are trouble. Please move to another house.'

Jack the Fibber turned up at my house a few months later. After being released from prison, he had been away on business in the Philippines. I was nervous as hell of seeing him, thinking that he might hold me responsible in some way for Barry's death, but he was fine. In fact, considering he had lost a son, he was extraordinarily laid back about the whole thing. He knew of Barry's habit and the autopsy had confirmed that the cause of death was an overdose of heroin. Jack insisted that I travel back to Manila with him, where he would introduce me to a few people that he felt would be good for my business.

The Philippines shares many characteristics with Thailand. Manila is like Bangkok. Corruption and prostitution are rife but so are energy, ingenuity and industry. The Filipinos are not quite so happy-go-lucky as the Thais are and there is an edge to the place. Nevertheless I liked the country as soon as I stepped out of the airport. Jack introduced me to a selection of Australian gangsters, drug dealers and petty criminals. Among them were Uncle Joe, who was a big-time drug dealer, and Neddy Smith who later became to

Australia what the Kray Twins were to Britain. They even made a film of his life called *Blue Murder*. Then, Neddy was a youngish man like myself, Uncle Joe and Jack were much older, and they got on well. Neddy laughed and joked a lot and he struck me as a lovable rogue; I found it hard to believe the stories I heard about him in later life when he was accused and imprisoned for cold-blooded murders and more.

What was immediately apparent, though, was that the Australians had a real foothold in Manila. They took me on a tour of bars in the red-light district, many of which they owned, and when we moved from one bar to the next, the busy street throng would part to allow us to walk around with a ring of personal space. People stared. Prostitutes did not approach unless asked. In the bars where they competed on 'concepts', Jack, Joe, Neddy and the others were treated like lords. One bar's concept was to cook omelettes for the punters with the novelty of the egg being secreted in a lady's crotch and it being cracked open in front of you by a contraction of her vaginal muscles. Another offered naked girls dancing around a cock-fighting pit: sex and violence co-existing in medieval harmony. The Aussies looked after me well and did not pressure me to do any particular business. I was glad of that because up until then, I had managed to steer clear of gangsters and organised crime and my self-preservation instinct told me to keep it that way.

Back in Thailand I started arranging a visit back to England, where I figured the police would have forgotten about me by now. They had Shergar to find for a start. I always used a little bucket-shop in a Bangkok back street for my travel arrangements. The Thai lady in there spoke near-perfect English and we became quite friendly. I think I had explained away my constant travelling to her with my soap powder marketing manager story. This time she asked me if I had any contacts in the food industry.

'Why's that?' I asked.

'Well, my husband, he has good job with Charapokapong Group

but he wants to leave and start own business in food export. He has some customers ready but he need £100,000 to start up and some more customers.'

I had been looking for a legitimate business in which to invest my money. This was a perennial problem for people in my industry – if you got hold of too much money, too quickly, and it was lying around, sooner or later people start asking questions. Unlike Howard and some other people I knew, I wasn't going to throw it away in lost causes close to my heart. I really wanted to make a legitimate fortune now.

'I'll give him the £100,000 for 50 per cent of the business,' I declared, overlooking the small fact that there was no business, yet.

'But you never meet my husband,' she replied incredulously.

'Do you trust him?'

'Yes.'

'Do you think he will be successful?'

'Yes.'

'Well, that's good enough for me.'

Mr Wanchai and I rented an office and called our newly registered company ToppFood International Trading Company; I don't believe I knew of Trotters Independent Trading Company at the time. Wanchai was fired up and I warmed to him straight off when he wrote to food importers around the world telling them of his new state-of-the-art food-canning factory. When we received an order from Germany for tinned tuna, Wanchai and I had to hurry out to the outskirts of Bangkok to find a factory owner who would allow us to masquerade as the proprietors for a few hours when the Germans visited for an inspection. This was not difficult. We got the best price out of the Germans and beat the Thai factory owner down as much as we could. The margin remaining was respectable. By the middle of 1983, orders were flying in and I found myself in the more comfortable position of sending tuna and pineapple chunks around the world rather than Thai sticks and Kashmir hash. We suffered a bit from overtrading (we couldn't get the money in quick enough to finance paying for the orders that were flooding in) and Wanchai and I realised we should really open our own factory. I invested a further £150,000.

Pao was happier now that I seemed to be at home more and was able to say 'Good day at the office?' when I arrived back at the house every afternoon. Also, fewer strange people were phoning and visiting. The death of Barry in her house had upset her no end and she blamed me for bringing these things on her. Women can become funny about things like that.

The business grew and flourished. I was able to take a salary and joined Wanchai in our sumptuous Bangkok office most days. We started to pay dividends to ourselves and I began to enjoy the life of an international businessman. Mr and Mrs Wanchai must have wondered what happened to my soap powder career. I told myself that doing all those cannabis deals was a means to an end and being a director and owner of ToppFood, a respected international business, was that end. In the immortal words of Arthur Daley, the world was my lobster.

PANACHE AND PEOPLE CARRIERS
– MANILA, PHILIPPINES

Looking back on it now, it is strange how people just walked into my life. One morning an Arab sheikh breezed into the ToppFood offices. His company had imported some tuna and other fish products from us and he was in the country visiting. Would we care to join him for lunch? He was dressed in Western clothes and exuded wealth and elegance with his Gucci suit, Rolex watch and bejewelled fingers. This was before widespread faking of designer names and if someone was wearing a Rolex, it *was* a Rolex. His rings would have come from Asprey's in London. His conversation was punctuated with Praise Allahs and Inshallahs and he twisted worry beads through his fingers constantly. Arabs were common in Thailand as trade between the two regions was quite strong. They could often be found in the bars, brothels and gambling dens. It always amused me how members of one of the world's most uncompromising religions were attracted to the seediest dens of iniquity in the world.

'Can you supply labour?' he enquired.

I thought he was going to order a plane-load of pineapple chunks. Abdul then explained about the huge demand for labour in Saudi and neighbouring kingdoms. He didn't put it like this but, basically, Saudis will not get their hands dirty and, being oil-rich, they have the luxury of being able to afford to get others to do it for them. They had already bought expertise in the form of managers, engineers and financiers from America and England. They had already imported many well-educated people from Pakistan and India to man their police forces, civil service and other infrastructure jobs, now they were looking for cheaper labour still to build their office blocks and dig their roads. Indian, Pakistani, Thai and Filipino men were starting to be flown in by the thousand as labourers and construction workers, and their womenfolk were following them over to become maids and general servants. Abdul said the market was due to explode and that at present it was very fragmented and ripe for streamlining and dominating.

'We don't but we can,' I told him.

The Sheikh invited Wanchai and me over to Saudi to see our marketplace first hand. We flew into Jeddah. I remember stepping off the plane on to the tarmac and feeling as if I had stepped into an oven. I was accustomed to the Thai sun but this was the most stifling heat I had experienced up to that point. Normally you develop a sweat; here I was dripping as I walked to the arrival lounge.

We were put up in the Sheraton Hotel and I was surrounded by boundless ostentation. In the lounge areas, Arab men sat in chairs that would have been thrones anywhere else in the world, taking coffee from richly decorated silver pots. These were the very early days of mobile phones and invariably they had these brick-sized devices clamped to their ears as they conducted animated telephone conversations. I wondered who they were talking to as they spoke loudly into their new toys and threaded worry beads through their fingers with their free hands.

In Thailand, everyone is rushing around; in Saudi, nobody is in a hurry to go anywhere. Drinks and food are served and eaten slowly and leisurely. People dawdle everywhere and it is possible for them to have three or four polite conversations on the journey from their seat in the lounge to the toilet. The Saudis have achieved something no other country has – they have purchased time for themselves and they are determined not to fill it. A few ladies scurried around the lobby area dressed entirely in black with just a hint of eyes peering out of their burkas. The difference in attitude to women between here and Thailand could have not been more pronounced. I was puzzled when I saw one of these women taking a photo of three of her friends outside the hotel. Huddled together they looked like a black blob. How would they tell each other apart? Not a lot of point in saying 'Smile please'.

Abdul showed us around town and we passed walled compounds where British and American expatriates were enclosed because neither culture wished to clash. There were small armies of Indians and Pakistanis digging roads in the searing heat. I couldn't help being reminded of a chain gang but Abdul assured us it was the best thing that could happen to these people who were toiling away.

'They normally stay two years. They are sponsored by a sheikh and he looks after them well. When they return home, they should have enough money to buy a small house or a piece of land. Everyone is happy.'

I had no reason to disbelieve him. Curiously, Abdul did not invite us to his house, although he drove up outside and showed it to us. It was a palace with a flat roof. It doesn't rain in Saudi. He did not introduce us to his wives.

Abdul then took us to his offices in a glass skyscraper in town. It occurred to me that he could be pulling the same scam as we did with the German tuna buyers but next to a life-size oil painting of King Faisal was one of himself and it was obvious that everyone in the office knew him well. After this, Abdul suggested we nip over to Bahrain to have an evening out. Bahrain, he said, was a better place than Saudi to entertain.

'There is a causeway opening soon to link our two countries but today we will have to hop on a plane.'

He booked us into The Diplomat Hotel in Manama for two nights, gave us some money, tipped us off about some places to see and then, strangely, left us to our own devices.

As we were sitting in the bar, a couple came in and started up a conversation. They were from Ireland (could be tricky) and had lived in the country for some five years. Aiden worked in a bank and Libby was a hostess for Gulf Air. Aiden was a scream and he started to tell us about life as an expatriate.

'We've just had the Hollies over and the island hasn't recovered yet. You see, nothing happens. So, for the expats at least, little inconsequential things take on enormous proportions.' Aiden said he worked for the biggest bank in the country but it was a doddle and they paid him a fortune.

'I'm in IT. When I flew over here, I'd never switched on a computer. Honest to God. Just bullshitted. There's no one here to prove you wrong. The place is teeming with Indians who are nothing short of computer geniuses. Just get them to do all the work and we take the credit. If you're English, you can do no wrong out here.'

'But you're Irish,' I pointed out.

'Same thing in Bahrain.'

He was very disparaging about the hosts who were lining his pockets.

'See, Brian, everything is back to front out here. Most countries build up industries to create wealth but British and American companies have found oil in the Gulf and the Arab countries that own the reserves are now rich beyond their wildest dreams, but they have nothing else apart from the money. So they are trying to create infrastructure and industries, but they don't know how. That's why they need the Indians and us. They love us but they treat the Indians like shit. My bank was only formed because they thought they should have a bank. It loses money hand over fist but they don't care – it's all about face on the world stage. Take this hotel. It's hardly ever full. People come here to talk but not many stay. But it will be subsidised in some way because they want the big hotel names here. The Arabs here love to think they are doing business but, of course, they are not. Very little business is actually done here.'

'Who are all those people rabbitting away to out there on their mobile phones then?' I enquired.

'Each other. Probably the bloke sitting next to him.'

I laughed.

'I'm serious,' said Aiden.

In the hotel room I switched the TV on and caught the news; actually there was nothing else on but the news. It consisted of items about the ruling Royal Family. Sheikh Hamad something or other visiting this school or taking coffee with the ambassador of a country I had never heard of. The footage was incredibly overlong, dwelling on the two men meeting, shaking hands, sitting down, taking coffee, sipping it and talking. The big news, though, was that Mrs Thatcher was flying over the country's airspace en route to somewhere else. The footage began with the King's entourage leaving the palace and getting into a fleet of cars to head towards the airport. The King sat in a chauffeur-driven, open-topped Buick, smiling broadly. At the airport they all assembled on the tarmac and looked to the skies, waving as a plane flew above them. I wondered if Maggie was waving back. I doubted it. You could have been forgiven for thinking the whole thing was a comedy sketch, especially as the background music throughout the entire news bulletin was the theme tune of *Monty Python's Flying Circus*.

The next day Aiden and Libby picked us up from the hotel in their Land-Rover, as they had offered to show us the sights. 'This will take about eight minutes,' said Aiden.

As we drove around, with him pointing out a bank here and an insurance company there, I mentioned the news I had watched and the Monty Python music.

Libby laughed.

'That's what Aiden was talking about yesterday. The television station is manned almost entirely by Brits but of course the Royal Family decide what goes on it. The Monty Python dubbing is the expats' idea of a laugh at their expense. That's their way of showing the expat community what a load of bollocks it is and that they don't take it seriously. The Arabs are none the wiser.'

'Sounds a bit risky to me.'

'Not really. The worst that can happen to you out here is getting packed off home. Actually the King is a great bloke. Would you like to meet him?'

'Don't tell me – he's a personal friend of yours?'

'Yes, he is.'

Aiden explained that the King had a private beach that he opened up only to Brits and Americans. His own people were not allowed on it and were not even supposed to know of its existence. Aiden said this was because if they saw the opulence in which he lived and that he was embracing parts of Western culture it would cause unrest.

'See, the country is rich for sure, but it hasn't trickled down everywhere yet.' I could see that. On the way to the beach I saw houses that were unfit for human habitation and the Mercedes cars of the city were replaced by donkeys.

The beach was not signposted in any way and was only reached by negotiating a number of dirt tracks after leaving the road. Armed soldiers guarded the entrance. There was a large sign saying NO CAMERAS. The sea was a lovely blue and the beach was fine yellow sand. Only a handful of people were around, mainly British and American women. Aiden pointed to a man in a silk Arab *thobe* sitting in a chair just a few feet away from the lapping sea. I was reminded of King Canute. A couple of beauties in bikinis sat around him. Soldiers standing either side of his throne handed out small bottles of 7UP as we approached.

'Good morning, Your Highness,' said Aiden. 'This is Mr Meehan and Mr Wanchai. They are doing business in Saudi Arabia.' The King and I indeed. I looked around for Jeremy Beadle.

Later I talked to our new friends about the manpower proposal we were looking at. He was philosophical. 'They have a shit life. You hear stories about them being on a two-year sponsorship but sometimes the sheikhs won't let them go. They are at the bottom of the pile here and all over the Middle East. The Arabs regard them as lower than their dogs. They work them like animals, pay them a pittance and make them sleep dozens together in old huts. The women have it a bit better. If they are a maid and they get a nice family then life can be pleasant. The best jobs for them, of course, would be with an expat. But they are limited. However, Brian, having said all that, it depends on what they are coming from. They pretty much know what they are letting themselves in for when they come. When they go home, they're not going to lie to their own people.'

For the first time I felt a bit uneasy about the manpower business. It was one thing packing up pineapple chunks or even Thai sticks and sending them all over the world, but human beings was another matter. In my eyes, the trade in cannabis was not immoral but it was illegal; however, the trade in people was not illegal but it may have been immoral.

We flew back to Saudi and I convinced myself of the merit in the latter part of Aiden's discourse. My doubts were more or less completely dissolved when he and Libby took us to their compound and we met his Filipino maid and Indian 'boy' (a servant-cum-gardener): they could have not been happier in their work. By the time Abdul introduced me to Dave, a pleasant young Englishman in his employ, I had convinced myself I would be performing a service for these people. Abdul invested £100,000 in ToppFood and sent Dave, who had come to the region as an air-conditioning man, back with us to develop our new manpower arm.

Dave suggested we explore the possibilities of sourcing our labour in the Philippines as the workers were even cheaper there and when I told him I had some contacts in Manila, he was delighted. I was wary about telling him exactly who these contacts were, however, as both he and his Arab boss had no idea of my other life. But as I got to know Dave well, I could see he was a man after my own heart: bent, unscrupulous and ambitious, with a love of a pound note.

I spoke to Jack the Fibber and he thought I was losing it when I told him I was pursuing a straight business. Nevertheless, he introduced me to two key contacts: Donna Price and Billie Jenkins. They were good-looking Aussie women, no longer in their prime, but still both classy and stylish ladies. Billie was, I was told, shagging the head of the Filipino Army and the Army was almost as powerful as President Marcos. People like Marcos had to keep the Army sweet. The Army kept the people in order, but upset the Army, and they could overthrow you. In these parts of the world this often happened. Therefore Billie was powerful. Donna was her best friend and she was in with Jack and the boys. Things were becoming clearer. Donna encouraged us to open an office in town and, to make sure we hung around, she introduced me to a beautiful Filipino girl who bore an uncanny resemblance to my ex-girlfriend Shirley. This should have turned me off but I ended up buying her a flat for us to live in when I was in the country.

'Now, I will introduce you to someone who will make business very profitable for you over here,' Donna said.

Surely the Aussie mob did not have their claws into Ferdinand Marcos himself? Maybe Imelda, his shoe-loving wife? No they didn't. But the bloke they did introduce me to was the next best thing.

I was invited to a party at a grand house called Alabang, which had previously been the Peruvian Embassy. As Donna took me through into the big reception room, a large, avuncular English gentleman bounded towards us clutching his champagne glass. A monocle would not have looked out of place squeezed into his eye. He looked like he could have been an English lord. He was.

'Philip, meet Lord Moynihan.'

'Call me Tony.'

That was handy because, as his business card stated, his full name was Lord Anthony Patrick Andrew Cairnes Berkeley Moynihan.

His history was sketchy and I could only piece it together from snippets provided by himself and stories told by those around him. He had inherited a baronetcy and was public-school educated, of course, in England. His father, the second Lord Moynihan, had died in 1965 while facing charges of homosexual importuning. Tony himself had been a bit of a rebel and had caused a society stir when he had married an exotic fire-eating dancer in the 1960s. Then a scandal blew up when he had to flee Britain following some allegations of fraud. I never really got to the bottom of what type of fraud it was but Moynihan did indicate once that he had bought a Rolls Royce from Jack Barclay's in London with a bouncing cheque. The press had dubbed him the 'Barmy Baron'.

For a time he took refuge in General Franco's Spain and then moved on to Australia. Here he must have met Jack the Fibber and the Aussie mob he seemed so attached to. His version was that he played bongos in a Sydney nightclub. On to the Philippines, where he had a range of business interests including nightclubs and brothels; somehow he had managed to get the ear of President Marcos and behaved like some sort of unofficial Minister of Foreign Investment. Preferably dodgy foreign investment with lots of kickbacks for the good Lord.

His half-brother was more famous in England. Colin Moynihan, who, unlike his sibling, was a very small man, had risen to prominence in the Thatcher Government. Well, he became the Minister of Sport eventually, or the 'Minister of Short' as *Private Eye* sometimes called him. His brother on the other side of the world must have been a great cause of worry for a man with serious political ambitions.

Lord Moynihan was interested in my activities in and out of Thailand. He said he wanted to 'move in'. His knowledge of the Thai language was however limited to an old proverb, 'Never teach a crocodile how to swim.' I would find out over time how apt that was.

Moynihan and I discussed business ideas. He guessed that, as the Aussies had introduced me, some of my ideas might involve the breaching of some international laws and he made no secret himself of the fact that he was dodgy. In fact he positively revelled in his own criminality. We discussed massage parlours and I mentioned that I thought that, in Thailand at least, there was a gap in the market for high-class massage parlours. Tourists were spoilt for choice but international businessmen are normally a little more discerning and may not welcome the idea of being waylaid on the streets of Bangkok. He slapped his thigh.

'A man after my own heart,' he boomed.

We arranged that he would fly in to Bangkok to discuss an idea of his along these lines in more detail at a later date.

A fortnight later, he and his entourage were swanning around Bangkok. We met at the prestigious Hyatt Central Plaza Hotel between the city and the airport. With him was a man who called himself James (as he was Thai, this was obviously not his real name), who was a property developer and hotel owner. According to Moynihan he had 'serious money' (Moynihan worshipped people with 'serious money') and also owned a number of department stores as well as a former Miss Thailand. Moynihan floated a plan to convert the basement of the very hotel where we were sitting into an in-hotel barber shop and massage parlour. It hadn't been done before. We'd employ the best girls, who'd be highly discreet. Male guests could tell their wives or girlfriends they were popping downstairs for a haircut and never would an item more incriminating than a barber shop charge appear on the bill. I added the innovation of regular guests using gold cards which could be handed out to particular people in Bangkok we needed to keep sweet. The Chief of Police sprang immediately to mind.

Moynihan's vision was a three-way equity split: him for having the idea and making the introductions, James for providing the working capital and ToppFood for an initial £10,000 investment, managing the project and then continuing to build and run the business. Later Moynihan asked me for a £25,000 up-front bung.

'Mr Philip, we need to have this basement stripped out, refurbished and open to the public in two months. Is this good? Has your company the experience of a project of such magnitude?' enquired James.

'Oh sure. It'll be tight but we can be open in eight weeks. No problem.'

Flesh was pressed and Lord Moynihan, James and a group of other men, whose purpose I know not, got up and left Dave and myself in the empty basement.

I looked at Dave and said, 'Know any builders?'

Dave, who was fast getting accustomed to my bullshit and was now surprised by nothing, stood there with his hands on his hips shaking his head.

'Well, there is Danny, an American builder we use out in the Middle East. He's good and he can run a team OK but he's used to serious money out there.'

'Well, we'll give him serious money here. Get him over here now.'

Danny duly arrived and set to his task at a furious pace. He worked wonders with the local timber and refurbished the place with a lovely teak wood. Behind the barber unit that fronted the shop he installed two beautiful marble baths that led on to the private rooms. One afternoon as we all toiled, three men wandered into the basement.

'Hi guys, just being nosey. What you building here?' Danny's mouth fell open, as did mine, when we looked up to see former US President Jimmy Carter and two bodyguards standing in the doorway. He was on an official visit of the region and was staying at the Hyatt.

'Just a concession,' I answered vaguely.

'Good handiwork.' He smiled broadly as he admired the finish. 'I'm a bit of a carpenter myself.' He chatted awhile with his fellow American, Danny, and told him he had started work as a chippie. Strange, I always thought he was a peanut farmer. I was tempted to invite him back when it was all finished but thought better of it.

Danny and Dave kept the whole project on course and when we were close to opening, I devoted myself to the far more arduous task of recruiting the girls. I was determined that we would use only the best girls and this place, whilst discreet, would establish itself as the most desirable massage parlour in Bangkok. I placed an advertisement in the *Bangkok Post* offering a salary of 30,000 Thai Baht a month. Normal working girls at the time would have averaged around 5,000 Baht and, to put this into perspective, a Bangkok bank manager would only have pulled in 25,000 Baht. My intention was to deter some of the more careworn working girls and to attract those ladies with bigger ideas, and perhaps tempt a few models or stunning students or shop assistants.

We asked applicants to arrive at our ToppFood offices on a Tuesday morning. I had suspected the response would be healthy but as I swung the car into our street bright and early, I was stunned to see a queue of girls and women snaking right down to the end of the road and around the corner. Fucking hell, I thought, I must start processing these girls before I have the police around demanding to know what's going on.

During the day 200 girls came upstairs to the office and we took them into a side room, asked them to undress and generally checked them over. It sounds sordid now but myself, a guy called George and a Filipino lady called Mona sat behind a desk and took details and made notes. It was a bit like *Pop Idol* without clothes. George was an American friend of ours who did nothing in particular but had the distinction of being the last American soldier to have been taken prisoner in the Vietnam War. Mona had been sent over from Manila by Lord Moynihan to oversee the selection process and give us general advice. She was an elegant and beautiful 35-year-old woman, who I imagine had started out as a working girl but was now running Moynihan's Manila brothels.

We whittled the first batch down to 40 and invited them back to a further 'interview', to take place a couple of days later at a so-called 'love hotel' we had hired for the purpose. The 40 remaining girls were all fabulous. Mona took control and explained the concept in detail: what would be required of the girls and how their earnings would be made up.

'If any of you don't do blow jobs, you'd best leave now.' George and myself stayed put but two or three of the girls quietly padded out the room.

'How many of you have done this before?' asked Mona. About half of them had, or admitted they had. Five or six said they hadn't had sex at all but elected to stay the course.

'Right,' said Mona, 'I'm going to give you a few tips. The more customers you do, the more money you will earn. However, never let the customer think you are rushing him. The trick is not to appear to be in a hurry but to make him come reasonably quickly. Phil or George, is one of you up for a bit of practical?'

One of the advantages of being an ex-soldier is that you learn to act decisively. I hesitated and George stepped forward, removing his trousers simultaneously. Mona laid him on the bed and liberated his penis from his underpants. She held it in one hand as she spoke to the girls. It was like a professor addressing a class of medical students. Two more girls slipped out of the door.

'Most of you know how to give a blow job, I'm sure,' she said, smiling as she popped George's member into her mouth. Don't teach the girls to suck eggs, I thought.

'But a little a bit of this can speed things up a bit,' she continued as she came up for air and rubbed along the shaft of George's penis with one hand whilst gently but firmly squeezing his bollocks with the other. She then disengaged from George and began chatting about love-making techniques and various other ruses to dispose of clients quickly and happily. Meanwhile George was still horizontal, his eyes rolling at the back of his head and arms and legs dangling off the side of the bed. When Mona finished lecturing, she looked behind at George and laughed. She pointed to two identical twins at the front of the class and said, 'Go on, finish him off, will you?'

One twin stripped off and sat on his groin area whilst the other jumped up on him and moved up towards the other end of his body. Sadly, Mona then ushered us out of the room.

All was set for the grand opening. We had christened the place Panache and had installed an Englishman as manager. He had a real

Oxbridge accent. The Thais and the hotel guests would love him. We invited anyone who was anyone in Bangkok, and had gold and silver cards printed which we handed out to senior policemen, bank managers, hotel officials and other key people. The gold cards entitled the owner to free membership and unlimited use of the parlour and silver gave half-price deals. We sweetened everyone we needed to. A prominent executive from Thai Airways was one of the first guests to arrive and he wasted no time in road-testing two girls.

Panache was a phenomenal success. International businessmen and visiting tourists lapped it up. We had fifteen girls on at all times and they managed to squeeze in nine or ten customers a day each. There were 300 rooms at the Hyatt so the girls were always kept busy. Our turnover and profits were way over all expectations, as were the earnings of the girls. In comparison to their downtown contemporaries they had won the lottery. Several of them retired after less than a year, having accumulated enough money for whatever it was they wanted to do with their lives.

Around 1986, the Manchester United team turned up for a pre-season tour. Unfortunately, what I know about football after England won the World Cup you can write on the back of a condom packet. I got a look at the players but didn't recognise any. I was hoping that George Best, Bobby Charlton or Denis Law might have held on till then but sadly not. Our English manager knew them though and was pointing them out to me as they came in and out of the hotel. In the foyer area of Panache we had a television and I was sitting in there once with Dave and our manager and some of the girls whilst United were playing a Thai side live on the TV. As the cameras closed in on specific players, the girls would squeal and giggle, 'He the man from here, I fuck him yesterday in his room', and, 'He very beeg.'

Another time, the American Dental Association had a convention at the Hyatt and their representative came to me and asked if we could supply a special guest. They wanted our best girl and they asked if they could cover her in a chocolate coating. This was not a problem. The girl told me after that she'd had to move among the dentists at their tables and they would lean forward and take a crafty lick of her naked, chocolate-covered body. They worked themselves up into a frenzy and finally she lay on the floor as the drunken dentists fought one another to devour every part of her body. I hope that English dentists wouldn't behave in such a fashion.

Tony, my brother, sent his son Dylan out to Bangkok for an extended holiday when he was 17. Dylan had hit that point in adolescence when he thought he was the bees' knees and, despite my attempts to chaperone him, he was having none of it. One evening, whilst drinking quietly in a bar, he was approached by a lady-boy. Dylan was ecstatic and was clasping his/her buttock in his hand whilst winking at me.

'I've pulled a cracker here, Phil.'

'Dylan, she's a boy.'

'Fuck off. Jealous, are we?'

I did my best to explain the real situation to him but he would have none of it. I turned to the lady-boy.

'You have cock?' I had to ask this, because some of them had had them chopped off. I motioned to her/him to lift his skirt. Sure enough, the male genitalia was there even if it was taped up between the legs.

Dylan was horrified.

'I told you, Dylan. Listen to your Uncle Philip. I live here. You'd probably get a great blow job but the problem is, when it's finished, she'll want you to give her one back.'

I took one huffy teenager back to Panache. Mona just happened to be in town. She must have been training up some new girls. Mona had an unusual theory on how to keep her skin looking young. She believed that the semen of teenage boys, preferably virgins, rubbed into her face was the key to eternal youth. Her skin was certainly beautiful and she was in better nick than many girls half her age. She looked at Dylan and a smile spread across her face.

'Mona, this is my nephew, Dylan. He's 17 years old.'

She didn't even reply but took a bemused Dylan by the hand and led him into one of the siderooms inside Panache.

Back in England, meanwhile, the wife of the marketing director of a leading pharmaceuticals multinational company was opening up the mail one morning over breakfast in Esher, Surrey. Her husband was engrossed in the *Financial Times*. She was studying an American Express credit card statement.

'Brian, you know when you went to Thailand on business earlier this month?'

'Yes, darling.' He hadn't looked up from his paper.

'Why did you get your hair cut seven times?'

HOWARD'S WAY
– VANCOUVER, CANADA

Looking back on it, I was at my peak. ToppFood was providing Wanchai and myself with a good honest living. The manpower side had really taken off and we were chartering planes galore packed solid with Filipinos bound for Saudi. Finally, Panache was so embarrassingly successful that it had become difficult to keep it discreet. Rumours had started that the girls were off-duty hostesses from Thai Airways and Singapore Airlines. Far-fetched I know, but it was a rumour I was quick not to deny. Our English manager had moved on and we had recruited a local lady who was just as effective. If I had wanted to, I could have flourished further without becoming involved in any more dope deals but I couldn't resist the odd dabble. People came to me and I suppose I got off on my reputation as being a reliable and skilled mover in the region. If someone wanted Thai grass, I was the man. Howard Marks, for example, was now just one of many fixers who came to me to source grass for deals. I enjoyed the challenge and the danger and I could not resist the easy money, the type of money that arrives in life-changing dollops.

These are the characteristics of a gambler. In a sense I was not much different from the men that came into my dad's and uncle's shops in the 1960s and gambled with the little money they had. The danger they courted was facing the wife after having done a week's wages, the challenge they sought was beating the bookmaker by selecting the correct horses, and the wins they sometimes enjoyed may not have been life-changing dollops but occasionally they were mouth-watering week- or month-changing amounts.

Around this time I was involved in a few medium-sized deals into Ireland. Howard Marks had opened up the market years before in the 1970s. This was a country where there was still a black market in condoms; it stood to reason that it would be some time before there was a serious market for puff. Howard had got involved with a guy called McCann who claimed to be in the IRA and gave the impression of being able to kill people at will and without retribution of any sort. He had Dublin Airport 'under his control' and had asked Howard for gear. Mr Nice obliged with some top-quality grass. This was McCann's first encounter with beneficial herbs and when he and his cohorts ripped open the first carton and pulled handfuls of weed out, they turned to Howard menacingly and shouted, 'This is grass.'

'That's true.'

A gun was cocked. Howard's smile vanished. He was forced to roll a joint and share it around among the sceptical Irishmen to convince them that the grass was grass and not grass. The IRA, who have always held strong views on all drugs – hard or soft – have always vehemently denied that McCann was ever a member of their organisation.

I was introduced to a confident young Englishman named Jason, who was very eager to get involved in some deals. I put him on to one whereby he would take a hired car into Ireland for a holiday. The car would have been packed up with some hash and not even Jason knew where it was concealed. Once in Ireland he was instructed to go to a certain place from where the car would be stolen. After a few hours, Jason would report the theft to the Gardai, who would subsequently find the car now lightened of its cargo. It was very easy and Jason did a couple more trips of a similar nature. What I didn't know was that back in his home town in the Midlands Jason was 'giving it large', as they say. Down his local social club he took to smoking large cigars, wearing chunky gold bracelets and boasting to anyone that would listen about his 'earners'. He stopped short of telling his drinking buddies exactly what his earners were. One fellow drinker was a former footballer who was a household name nationally and a hero locally and had gone as far in his career as playing for his country in the World Cup finals. Even I remembered his name from my schooldays. Jason persuaded him to come along on the next trip and the soccer star went for the break. I honestly believe he had no idea what he was letting himself in for. The world where he had grown up in the industrial Midlands was a very different one from the one the likes of Jason and I populated. This time Jason was captured importing cannabis into Ireland and he and the unlucky former international footballer were hauled before the courts, where they received prison sentences. We tried to supply money to their families whilst they were incarcerated but they were understandably not interested in our charity or guilt money.

It is a fact that the peripheries of the drug smuggling trade attract people like our aforementioned actor and ex-footballers. They can be respectable people who have enjoyed some financial success and have become accustomed to a certain kind of lifestyle. They often find themselves without a career and, more importantly, an income, at a time of life when it is hard to break into a normal career path. Failed businessmen are another group that can sometimes gravitate towards the drug scene. In their own way and on a different level, perhaps they had become as desperate as the Third World 'mules' that are continually exploited by small-time drug traffickers the world over. And, of course, these people were perfect for carting money around the world on behalf of people like Howard and myself. It would be folly to use anyone that looked like a drug user or fitted any of the social stereotypes of one. Howard Marks himself, the eternal hippie, was the exception to this rule but then again he rarely got his hands dirty these days.

Howard came to see me around this time in the mid-1980s. Shortly before, he had invited me over to London to attend the grand opening of one of his legitimate companies. We had dinner with the Chinese Ambassador to Britain and an MP and cabinet minister named Peter Brooke. Howard reckoned that Customs and Excise fell under his portfolio and he thought this was hilarious. This was the sort of thing we did to crack each other up. If the minister knew he was dining with two drug-smuggling fugitives he would have choked on his barbecued ribs and that was the joke.

We had not worked together for some time, me having gone my own way and him spending some time in prison. He had been arrested in 1980 for, among other things, importing 15 tons of Colombian marijuana from the United States to Britain. The trial that ensued in 1981 restored Howard to the front pages of the newspapers and was his moment of triumph. He mixed truth with fiction to create a cocktail of stories that encompassed his recruitment into MI6 and their instruction for him to infiltrate the IRA. He also revealed how he was recruited by the Mexican secret service to infiltrate the IRA. Confused? So were the jury. A whole web of politics and intrigue was woven cleverly by Howard and everyone, including the jury, was left thoroughly baffled. His charm won the day and, after an expensive trial lasting some months, he was found not guilty. As far as I could make out, Howard's involvement with the security services didn't go much further than an approach, years ago, from a former university chum who now had a career with MI6. But, of course, Howard had signed the Official Secrets Act so he can't tell us much more, can he? Personally Mr Nice struck me as more MFI than MI5.

Howard was a free man again by May 1982; he had served some time on other lesser charges, but it was generally considered that he had beaten the system. It was probably then that the Americans decided that if the English could not, or would not, nail this man, then they would. He was an internationally notorious figure whose Robin Hood status was growing by the minute and, with hindsight, anyone who was still in the business should not have gone near him with a barge pole. But Howard was fun. And if you cannot enjoy your work, why bother?

When he came over to Thailand after our London meal, he

brought over two men he wanted me to meet. Howard was a great one for networking. They were a couple of south London criminals, dare I say gangsters? They were in their 50s and 60s and both had the air of men who had spent considerable time in prison. They were dressed immaculately and had some style but pulled cigarette-rolling machines from their pockets after dinner. The older one clearly found it difficult to suppress the violence that bubbled under the charming exterior. When he shook my hand, he crushed it in a friendly way. When he looked at me as he talked, the look was just that little bit too intense and a little bit too lingering. The slightly younger one was just a maniac who was wolfing his food down and wishing the conversation would end so he could get outside and sample the Bangkok nightlife. I wondered what Howard was playing at, involving himself, and more crucially me, with these sorts of people. Especially when I ran the older man's name through my mental indexing system and could remember it as one that I had seen from time to time in the Sunday tabloids back at home years before in connection with armed robbery gangs. Perhaps Howard had made a new type of friend during his time in prison?

The gist of the conversation was that these chaps wanted to get involved in the drugs business and they understood we had been doing rather well in it for some time, so maybe they could learn a thing or two from us. They said they had no intention of muscling in on us but we didn't own the trade and there was room for everyone. Quite. I had never thought in terms of market share or worried about what other people were doing and I am sure Howard was the same. Despite the claims that would surface later that our 'network' was responsible for a significant percentage of the world's drugs trade and we 'controlled' the industry, we were just a bunch of guys doing some deals. Big deals, I grant you, but the notion we controlled anything other than ourselves and the deal in question at the time was nonsense. And as a percentage of drugs that were winging or sailing their way around the world at any one time, we were still small beer. Organised crime gangs such as the Mafia were the big boys and they made no distinction between puff or heroin and cocaine, unlike ourselves and many other smaller players.

Howard was playing the genial host and as the drink flowed we regaled them with a few stories about the fun and games we had got up to in our time. Suddenly the older man turned to us and his eyes burnt into me.

'Cunts like you make me sick.' He was gripping his wine glass by the neck so tightly I thought the bowl would break off. If it did, I was close enough for him to jam it into my face. This was the sort of danger I did not relish. Now he is going to demand money with menaces, I thought.

'I have spent more of my life in nick than out. Me and my generation have been running around holding up post offices and banks for three fucking grand and drawing 15-year stretches for our efforts. You bastards leave fifty grand in a Tesco bag under your bed and forget about it. It's a joke. Bunch of fucking 'ippies an' all. We should have been robbing you fuckers. Not the fucking post office or the Nat fucking West. You'd have shit yourself and given it to us anyway. I don't expect you've ever seen a sawn-off shotgun in your lives?'

We shook our heads. I hoped he was not about to produce one. (Hippy? Me?) He was very angry but I was relieved when I realised that his anger was directed at his situation rather than us. He had a point. If TV business gurus John Harvey-Jones or Gerry Robinson had come to them with the offer of an analysis of their business, they would have concluded that the risk–reward ratio was far too low. Robbing a bank or post office was not likely to yield more than £10–20,000 for the robbers. Normally there would be two or three of them to share the proceeds and the chances of being caught were high. As they all found out in the end, the sentences of seven years or more were quite severe.

The risk–reward ratio in our game was a whole different ball game. People at the bottom of the chain, those who were dropping a bit of money here and there, were earning more than these bank robbers. Therefore the potential financial rewards were enormous and although prison sentencing was more severe (indeed in some countries there was an outside chance of execution), the chances of getting caught were slim. For every 'drug baron' and 'drug gang' you hear about being busted, there are thousands of people operating who have never been caught. There are even more people around who have done a one-off consignment to pay for a house or a car or to pay a VAT bill and have left it at that. Just as the percentage of the population under 60 years of age who have smoked grass at some time is far higher than is admitted to (I would estimate 50 per cent), the number of people that have crossed a border with an illegal drug is also enormous. Our south London guest was angry about opportunities wasted and a life lost.

The two men opened up a route between Thailand and England for Thai sticks, which I have to say was ingenious but simple. I wish I could tell you about it but it is not my copyright and I am loath to break any confidences. They had a method of getting the sticks in at the other end that was foolproof in terms of the entry and not getting caught. I always kicked myself for not thinking of it, as I did about the board game Trivial Pursuit, incidentally. That was my idea, I just hadn't got around to thinking of it.

Howard and I willingly introduced them to people in official places at our end and other vital cogs in the machine in Thailand and around, and left them to it. Sadly, despite the great system, they got busted. And it was down to two things: greed and lack of common sense. They were doing load after load and earning more money than they ever had before, yet they chose to dispense with our advice and contacts, resenting, I expect, the concept of anyone getting anything for nothing (in their eyes). After we were out of the picture they replaced all our people at the Thai end with their own. Suddenly the chain had been weakened tremendously. Back at home the older man moved from his semi-detached house in London and bought a huge gaff in the Surrey stockbroker belt. He traded in his old Jag for a Bentley. His younger accomplice had decamped to Spain, bought a Porsche and lived the high life with a bevy of young beauties on his arm. Both men purchased racehorses and paraded themselves at courses up and down the country. As they were well known to the police, they couldn't have told them more clearly 'Look lads, we're having it right off.'

Nothing winds an English detective up more than seeing their adversaries getting beyond themselves. They don't even like you if you earn more money than them and, let's face it, most people do. Both men and the rest of their gang received hefty prison sentences. The older man could be in his 80s when he is released. The saddest thing is there was no need for them to have been caught.

This is the fundamental problem with organised crime – criminals organise it. If only the industry could attract more straight people, it would function much better. To operate effectively you need to recognise that basic business and management principles apply. You need to incentivise your staff, you need to give your suppliers good deals, you need to adapt to the external environmental factors (bribe the right people), you need to price competitively, you need to build long-term relationships. If you apply the laws of the London or New York mean streets to big business, legitimate or illegitimate, it will undoubtedly fail.

Soon Howard and I were involved in quite a bit of business again. I was now in a position to put business *his* way. We used each other and worked independently as well. He was surprised by how well I was doing and the size and volume of deals I was executing. He couldn't believe I had reached this point whilst remaining essentially an independent. Howard was also fascinated by my legitimate interests. He even took a share in Panache. He loved that concept. Howard himself had some legitimate companies, including a travel agency in Piccadilly, London, and was interested in securing a deal with Philippine Airways for preferential tickets and rates. His business card pictured a kite flying high. Very Howard.

'Do you know anyone in the Philippines who can pull any strings?' Howard enquired of me one day.

'I know the chief fucking puppeteer,' I said.

Lord Moynihan was as excited about me introducing him to Howard as Howard was about meeting him. Moynihan had read a book about Howard and believed all the bullshit about his power, connections in high places and money. They got on like a house on fire. Because Howard was well-educated, well-read and well-off (so was I, I just didn't let the likes of Moynihan know too much), he appealed to the snob in Moynihan. Howard could not have been more impressed with Moynihan, for the Lord had also brought a head of Philippine Airways to his little welcome cocktail party. Moynihan, Howard and myself cooked up a number of business ventures that night as we demolished wine that, according to the Lord, was older than Queen Victoria. It tasted like Black Tower to my uneducated palate. The three of us did eventually open a non-sex nightclub in the Patpong area of Bangkok — which was a novelty in itself.

Moynihan wanted to impress Howard and invited us to travel with him to the Ilocos Norte region of the Philippines, where Rocky Ablan, a close confidante of President Marcos, was the Vice-Governor and was having a party. Indeed, it was a party held in his honour and was called 'Ablan Day'. Rocky's father was a national hero, having been the leader of the Resistance movement during the Japanese occupation of the Philippines, and the people still celebrated his life every year. Naturally, Rocky was the VIP guest.

We travelled on a small plane, the likes of which I had never seen before and haven't since. It was a bumpy 300-mile trip with the plane making all manner of throaty engine noises, and the laughing pilot seemed to be struggling with the controls to maintain an even course. Howard was shitting himself. He had a degree in physics and he always said that planes staying in the sky defied scientific laws. He was concerned that this trip could prove his contention. What was particularly noticeable about the plane was the way in which it landed. It basically hovered over the area on which it wanted to land and then dropped like a stone with a big bump. Excuse the pun, but it was like a sparrowhawk dropping on its prey. It was truly surreal. When we got to the party, we all needed a drink, Howard more than most.

Things didn't improve for him. The region was like the Wild West of America and the local mayors were the equivalent of sheriffs, walking around with guns and holsters and dispensing justice when they saw fit. Howard fell into a drunken conversation with one such mayor about his shooting prowess and I couldn't believe my eyes when he agreed to stand by the lapping sea with his arm stretched away from his body, gripping a bottle that the mayor promptly shot from his hand. The things we do under the influence of drink.

Another former pop star came on the scene around this time, although I don't think Howard would have had aspirations to manage him. He was yet another 'contact' Lord Moynihan introduced me to. 'Philip, you remember Frederick.'

This was Moynihan's code for – this man is or was famous. Frederick was one half of the German singing duo Nina and Frederick. I think they were in the Eurovision Song Contest one year, although it wasn't necessarily that which turned Fred to drugs. They had enjoyed some success in Britain and I had heard of them and their song 'Little Donkey' that had charted in the mid-'60s. My vague memory was that he looked a bit like Richard Stilgoe and she (Nina) had long blonde hair.

Frederick was actually Baron Frederick Von Pallandt and Nina his then wife. Ironically, one of the songs that made them famous dealt with the subject of puff. But this Puff was a magic dragon that lived by the sea. Fred's royalties had yielded enough for him to pursue business interests once the pop career had fizzled out. For a while he owned the famous directory of the aristocracy, *Burke's Peerage*, but I believe he sold it on. Maybe he looked Moynihan up in it, because they certainly had business connections. When I met him, he had a decent sort of boat and was using that to do fair-size loads in and out of wherever he could. Sometimes we overlapped with our various cargoes. He'd come a long way from standing on the revolving stage at the London Palladium waving to the audience at the end of the 1961 Royal Command Performance.

Moynihan's circle of friends was extraordinary. He claimed to have been a close friend of Ronald and Reginald Kray, though this probably meant that he had visited their Double R club one night. Thuggery and buggery he called them, but not to their faces, I'm sure. In Spain he had befriended Billy Hill, another old-time gangster. He spoke with fondness of Peter Rachman, saying he had been like a father to him. Rachman had been a slum landlord who wasn't opposed to arranging a spot of violence for non-compliant tenants and had been grilled by David Frost on a memorable television interview. Britain reviled Rachman — his name has even entered the dictionary as a word to describe exploitative landlords — yet Moynihan thought him kind and gentle.

He craved the company of criminals and their ilk yet conversely he had rubbed shoulders with many of the leading British establishment figures of the 1950 and '60s. According to Moynihan, everyone in the higher echelons of British society was a homosexual, a pervert or a spy. I dismissed most of this as fantasy, a sort of self-justification about his own chequered history, but have to admit that some of the things he confided to us and we dismissed as nonsense have since emerged as quite true. For example, he claimed Prince Charles had a mistress at the time when the Charles and Diana fairy-tale was still being played out and no such inkling had reached the public domain. Moynihan was resolute that Lord Lucan, 'the errant earl', who had disappeared after the murder of his children's nanny, was lying at the bottom of the English channel, not living under a new identity in South America or anywhere else as has been popularly believed.

At one of his cocktail parties he proudly introduced me to a man who wore his hair far too long for a man of his advancing years.

'Philip, meet Ronald Milhench. You must remember Ron.' I did remember the name but wasn't sure from where. Milhench was such a juicy, gangsterish name it sort of stuck in the mind. Ron could see though that I was struggling to recall where I knew him from.

'I had a bit of trouble with Harold Wilson a few years ago,' he grinned.

Then it all came back. For a while in 1974 his name was plastered over our newspapers at home and his face all over our television screens. It was the days of big hair, big collars and big ties. He forged the then Prime Minister Harold Wilson's signature to encourage potential backers for a property deal he was involved in. Ronald had run into financial difficulties after selling his insurance company some years before. Tragically his wife had earlier drowned when a car he was driving crashed into a Staffordshire lake. Milhench was not accused of any foul play in this incident even though it emerged that insurance cover on her life had been increased shortly before.

Harold Wilson had a history of becoming embroiled with some suspect names during his premiership, most memorably John Poulson, Lord Kagan of the Gannex raincoat empire and T. Dan Smith, but the Milhench affair was possibly the most damaging to the Prime Minister. The Wilson forgery earned Ron a three-year prison sentence. What exactly he was doing in Manila wasn't clear but he was a regular at Moynihan's little soirées.

I always remember that, like me, Moynihan had a penchant for false passports. The one he flourished in front of me bore the name of a William Kerr — it should have been Wayne Kerr.

Identity is something we take for granted. It is strange, but once you have changed it, you realise that it is not what it seems. It's just a label. A means of classification. It doesn't have to be permanent. When I was travelling as Brian Meehan, I thought I was him. Philip Sparrowhawk was someone else, someone I used to be in my childhood and youth. Although it is generally discouraged by governments, you can be anyone you want. It makes it difficult for the authorities to keep tabs on people and that is why they don't like it, but you really can change your identity if you wish. It is easy and in most cases not even illegal. When you hear about all these missing persons, very few of them have fallen victim to foul play, as is often our first thought. The vast majority have merely become someone else. We can change houses, change jobs, make fresh starts. Why not change who you are, if you fancy it?

By 1987, I had adopted the persona of another Irishman called Daniel Hamrogue. Brian Meehan had to go. He had given me a hard time what with all that St Patrick's Day palaver. Daniel Hamrogue would fare much worse.

Back in Bangkok, James, Moynihan's hotel magnate friend, was so pleased with how I had got Panache off the ground so quickly and so successfully that he started to recommend me to his friends in high places. He was instrumental in me brokering a deal with the Thai police for bullet-proof vests. I sold them 3,000 with a healthy mark-up on the deal. I sourced the vests from the United States and had cheekily asked if there were any 'seconds' that I could buy but there were not. It was also through James that I met an Israeli Army man who asked whether I knew anyone that might be interested in buying laser-guided mortar bombs.

'I'll ask around,' I said. I didn't fancy getting involved in that one. I later learned the chap's name was Colonel Gareth and he worked for Mossad, the Israeli intelligence agency. To this day I have never understood what that was all about.

James also put the Thai Army on to me. Was I the only person who could do deals in this part of the world? They wanted new gun barrels for their tanks. The manufacturer of the original barrels had gone bust years before and now they needed replacing. I needed to find a manufacturer who could take the specification and make new ones. I telexed all around the world but to no avail. I even held out the carrot of saying that I represented the Chinese military too, trying to make these manufacturers believe bigger orders would be in the pipeline. I think they knew that the Chinese had rather more modern military hardware however. Finally I received a reply from an Australian government body keen to attract trade and they invited me Down Under to take a look around a selection of factories.

I took Dave along with me for the Australian trip to source the gun barrels for the Thai army but did not tell him I was also picking up a tidy sum in commission at the same time for a load of hash I had sent down earlier. At Sydney airport, Dave and I were standing at baggage reclaim waiting for our luggage when four or five Customs men strode over and practically frog-marched us away. We were strip-searched and our luggage was taken apart. Barely a word was spoken. When they looked into my briefcase and found the papers pertaining to the gun barrels accompanied by an invitation from the Australian Government, they let us go. There was no apology though.

I knew now that something was seriously amiss. This kind of reception meant I was definitely on someone's radar and I could be pretty certain that we would be followed. How would I get hold of my money? How would I get it out of Australia? My sources had been warning me that the US campaign to nick Howard had been gathering pace and that I should be careful. Only now did I realise that I was being seriously targeted too.

I rang poor old Danny in Bangkok from my hotel and told him to fly from Bangkok into Sydney. When he arrived I called his hotel from my hotel and asked him if he would mind taking A$100,000 out the country for me.

'No, I fucking well won't, Phil. I'm a simple builder. I want no part in any of your deals. How dare you compromise me like this?' He was really, really angry. Danny was straight as a die and sometimes I forgot that most people are.

'Danny, keep your hair on, I was only joking.'

I wasn't. However, there was no point in taking silly risks so I wrote the money off for the time being and returned to Bangkok. Danny returned a day later absolutely hopping mad and trembling with fear and rage. He had been turned over good and proper by the Customs at Sydney on the way out. Never had he been so humiliated. It was probably the first time he had been asked to open his buttocks for a stranger to have a look up. This proved they were tapping our phones and had tuned in to my call to Danny, and the Australians, for one, were definitely on to us. I suspected that as the DEA were so keen to catch Howard they were now watching my every move and would have alerted the Australian authorities to my entry into their country.

If my first chance to alter the course of my destiny had been when my legitimate businesses were generating enough money to keep me in the style I was accustomed to, the Australian scare was my second. If I'd stopped my activities there and then I possibly could have saved myself. (I got the gun barrels ordered by the way.) Instead, perversely, I seemed to build up momentum. Howard and I went to Pakistan, where we had befriended a Government minister, and visited some hash-growing regions. This was part of my ambition to move to the top of the chain and into manufacturing, growing.

Parts of the country were very lawless and we were advised to hire armed bodyguards for our personal safety. Pakistan is one of the few countries I did not take to. There was no alcohol and the only working girls were kept in cages on the streets. I found it hostile and depressing.

From there we travelled to Manila for a meet with our old mate Moynihan. His extraordinary power was brought home to us when our plane landed at Manila airport and we taxied to the end of the runway. The stairs were lowered and we were allowed to drive off in a waiting car and out into the city. No customs. No passport control. We talked about some serious farming of weed out in the Philippine mountains funded by Government grants. We all felt extraordinarily powerful. Some governments were pursuing us but others were cooperating, even encouraging us. What we failed to understand fully was that in this world we live in today, only one government really matters.

Moynihan may have been a lord but he was never a government minister like myself. You don't believe me? Want a bet? I served as Consul General to the Kingdom of Thailand in the first Government of the Maori Kingdom of Tetiti. It happened like this. One of the few straight people who turned up at Moynihan's palatial home once was a man whose name I have forgotten, or rather whose name I could not pronounce so didn't bother learning, but who was the self-styled King of the Maoris. Like the Aborigines and the Native Americans, the Maoris were the indigenous race in New Zealand but had their homeland taken from them when the New Zealand islands were invaded by the white man. In more recent times the

Government had tried to assuage its guilt by giving a cluster of volcanic islands off the coast over to the Maoris for their very own. Big fucking deal. According to the King, the islands were useless and unfit for construction, humans and even sheep. All they had going for them, he said, was that they were an officially constituted kingdom and could issue their own passports. Passports? Howard and I were sympathetic to the Maori plight but suddenly this conversation had become even more interesting. Passports were always interesting to us. Diplomatic passports doubly so.

The King felt that if other countries recognised Tetiti, volcanic useless lumps of rock or not, the Maori people might start to get a seat at the top table.

'We can sort that out for you,' said Howard. 'Fidel for one would be delighted to recognise your country. He'd be very sympathetic, I assure you.'

Fidel? I knew Howard smoked some pretty strong grass but now he was on first-name terms with the President of Cuba? If you can't beat them, join them.

'And I'm pretty thick with some ministers back in Thailand; I'm sure I could push things along there. We are both well in with the Pakistan government and Tony still has influence in England.'

Howard nodded his head as vigorously as Howard can, and we were off and running. The King couldn't believe his luck meeting such a pair of movers and shakers, and a few weeks later he duly issued us with our official, totally legal diplomatic passports. I was honoured to look inside and see that I had been appointed Consul General to the Kingdom of Thailand. I think Howard may have been Minister for Propaganda.

My tenure in the Cabinet fizzled out after we really put Tetiti on the map but not in the way the Maori people particularly wanted. Howard went to Taiwan, mainly to size the place up because it was one of the few tolerable countries that did not have an extradition treaty with America or Britain and you never knew when we might need it. There he met an industrialist who complained to him about the current difficulty in dumping nuclear waste. For some reason nobody wanted it. Howard had an idea and called me. I called the King. Why didn't Tetiti accept people's nuclear waste for a fee? He was up for it and Howard negotiated a fee of $1 million for the first consignment. I told the King his exchequer would receive $250,000. He was happy, Howard and I were very happy and the nuclear waste company was ecstatic. We then went on to set up similar deals with other companies. They were countries really but they couldn't be seen to be dealing with nuclear waste and if it came on top, the country could blame the company.

The first consignment was steaming across the ocean in the direction of New Zealand when one of the other companies contacted the New Zealand Government. They couldn't really believe they would be acquiescent to all this. They were correct. When the Government realised what was happening they went ape-shit and dispatched their Navy to blockade the islands. Suddenly you couldn't move off New Zealand for frigates and gunboats. Greenpeace got to hear about it and sent a ship and protested loudly. On this side of the world it was headline news and I couldn't believe the stir we had caused. The nuclear waste was turned around, all other contracts were cancelled and an incensed New Zealand Government summoned the King to a meeting to rethink the whole question of Tetiti. It was time for Howard and I to resign our posts and seek new challenges.

Our dealings with Lord Tony Moynihan were soon throwing up such challenges. President Ferdinand Marcos had been deposed in a bloodless coup in 1986 amid much furore about his wife Imelda's collection of footwear. The lord became more edgy after that happened, although he did manage to survive under Cory Aquino, Marcos's successor. He felt vulnerable. His power base had been weakened and his quest for wealth became all the more urgent. He became even more Machiavellian, telling Howard not to trust me and vice versa. We both knew he was a crank and were therefore not unduly alarmed until one particular Manila visit.

Lord Moynihan's driver had taken us out for a tour of Manila's bars. We all became very drunk and the driver started to unburden himself about his employer.

'You must not trust him,' he implored.

'We don't.' We tried to laugh it off but the driver was insistent.

'Do you know where his big money comes from? He is trafficking heroin from the Philippines into Australia. That is bad. He bad, bad man. He is also informer.'

'Who does he grass to?' I asked.

'Anyone that will pay him.'

I don't think either of us ever trusted Moynihan. Howard and I didn't even trust one another. We all scammed one another on deals. But we would never set anyone up. I think we both made mental notes to move away from His Lordshit after that but events from then on moved so fast we were like rabbits caught in the headlights of a car at night on a country road. The notion that Moynihan was a grass was pretty scary stuff and it got scarier and scarier, pretty bloody quickly. People started to die.

The driver, full of alcoholic remorse, went back to his employer and confessed to his indiscretion. A few weeks later he was dead. According to Lord Moynihan, from food poisoning. Lead poisoning more like. We heard later that Moynihan had hired an Australian hit man named Parry to take the man out. Parry himself met a grisly end when he was taken up in an army helicopter and set about by some hired assassins who proceeded to chainsaw his head, arms and legs off before chucking them and the torso into the sea from a great height. But I get ahead of myself; we didn't know this yet.

If I had, I would not have gone for a drink with Robert Waldron. Robert worked out of Hong Kong and had the misfortune of marrying an ex-wife of Moynihan's. Moynihan had a few. He and Waldron did not like one another but seemed to do some business together and tolerate each other. This night in the bar, Robert was the second person in a matter of days to tell me to be very careful of Moynihan. When we left the bar, I hailed a cab to drop Robert off at his hotel and then take me on to my apartment. As I stepped into the road and raised my arm, I heard and smelt gunfire. I jumped out of my skin. Robert was lying on the pavement behind me. I glimpsed the man who had shot him as he calmly walked away and disappeared into the night crowd. Robert had been shot three times. He lived on for a few hours but tragically died later in hospital.

That shook me up. It was the first murder I had personally witnessed and I hoped it would be the last but amazingly I still didn't fully accept that Moynihan was behind these events. I didn't even consider myself in personal danger. With hindsight things were coming to a head.

In a catalogue of increasingly strange episodes around this period, just as the end was nearing, came the strange case of the pink nuns and the gold Buddha. The Hong Kong and Shanghai Banking Corporation had a merchant banking arm called Wardley. One of their executives was an old Etonian and I got pally with him after meeting on the Moynihan Manila dinner-party circuit. One evening he imparted to me the most intriguing story. He knew a Portguese-Filipino man called Ronaldo. Ronaldo's brother was a steamroller driver who had been working in the Davao area of the Philippines. During some tarmacking work he had unearthed a gold Buddha statue weighing a ton and a half. He rang his brother excitedly and told him about it. He said he was going to tarmac over the site because it was too dangerous to try and take the Buddha out without protection, and would be in touch with a view to his brother and other members of the family coming back and taking the Buddha at some later date. He told his brother that the building site was next to a convent that housed the Order of the Pink Nuns. This was becoming real *Raiders of the Lost Ark* stuff. Blue Nun was a cheap wine much imbibed by the aspiring middle classes back in the 1970s. Pink Nun was a new one on me.

These gold Buddhas are a big thing in the Philippines and every few years speculation flares up about them. It is a fact that when

General Yamashita marched through the Far East during the Second World War, his army plundered diamonds, gold and jewellery from wherever they could. It is said that this booty was stored in 16 of these gold Buddhas and buried hurriedly in different parts of the Philippines for recovery at some later date. Soldiers who worked for the Japanese general have testified to this. The banker was suggesting that now might be that later date. President Marcos of the Philippines was widely believed to have muscled in on one previous find and kept the riches inside the Buddha for himself.

What made the story especially interesting was that a day or two after Ronaldo's call from his brother, he had another call to tell him that his brother was dead. His body had been discovered by the roadside with his head caved in. Ronaldo was convinced that his brother's murder was linked to the gold Buddha and felt strongly that he had confided in someone and they had beaten him to death to make him say where the Buddha was. This was a reasonable assumption. Alternatively he could have shown someone and they had removed the Buddha and killed Ronaldo in the process. There was also an outside chance that his murder had no connection with the Buddha at all. People were routinely robbed and murdered in that part of the country. You could get your head cut off for a packet of Swan Vestas up there.

Nevertheless, I felt this was worthy of further investigation. Myself, Dave, Moynihan and Ronaldo took a private plane up to Davao and booked into the Intercontinental Hotel. Sure enough, the first taxi driver I asked if he knew a convent where pink nuns lived was able to help us out. It was some way up country but he was willing to take us. Moynihan refused to come, saying that it was too dangerous until we had arranged some protection from the people in the nearest village. Excited by this modern-day treasure-hunt, the rest of us couldn't wait and we piled into the old taxi. When the car pulled up by the old convent, my stomach flipped as I noticed that the tarmac we had pulled up on was freshly laid. A lady dressed as a nun, but all in pink, came out to meet us. This was definitely the place.

'Do you mind if we just have a look around? We're interested in old convents, you see.' Ronaldo was getting very nervous but Mother Superior was relaxed.

'Have you had some building work done here?' Dave blurted out.

'Yes. We have had the outer walls repaired and had this car park lain. It's just been finished.'

Dave and I started to talk excitedly out of the nun's earshot.

'This is the place.'

'Too right.'

'We'd have this tarmac up in no time.'

'We'd have to do it properly though.'

'What do you mean?'

'Well, we'd need to come in by boat in that bay there. We'd need to bring the digger and labourers in and we'd need a good 20 soldiers to guard us and help us get away.'

'What about the nuns?' asked Dave.

'If they know what's good for them they'll stay inside and shut up.'

'If not?'

'Well, if the worst comes to the worst, we'll just have to shoot them.'

That last statement was a joke for Dave's benefit but Ronaldo was becoming increasingly agitated and my flippant remark was the final straw. He ran off to the waiting taxi and left us high and dry. His brother had been slaughtered just down the road remember. Believe it or not the nuns phoned us a cab and Dave and I travelled back to the hotel full of plans and hope. Before we could get it together, though, events started to overtake us.

The operation to excavate a car park in a particularly unruly part of the Philippines, next to holy ground, would have been a sensitive and dangerous operation. But Dave and I were convinced it was possible. However, it had to be executed rapidly and would take careful planning and a great many palms being greased in the right places. Moynihan's contacts would be vital. But uncharacteristically, with such potentially large sums of money at stake, Moynihan was not focused on taking the quest further. He had other things on his mind and the possibly spurious pursuit of gold Buddhas was not one of them.

I didn't feel like continuing the quest for buried treasure with Lord Moynihan either once Tim Munday revealed to Howard and myself, shortly after the Pink Nun interlude, that Moynihan was now on the payroll of the DEA and had agreed to help them trap us. This confirmed our worst fears about him. Tim had worked with Howard for years, and had been the man who liaised with me in Hong Kong when I had my brush with the Children of God. He was now working with the DEA. Fortunately, he was working as a double agent, if you like, and was also feeding information to us. Unfortunately, he was also working as a double, double agent but we did not know that at the time. Basically, he was selling information about us, and the DEA, to whoever paid him. Tim informed us in detail how Moynihan was a grass and had been tasked by the DEA to accumulate evidence to convict Howard and all those who dealt with him. To this day I do not know what his motives were. He still felt nervy with his old mates Mr and Mrs Marcos living in exile on Hawaii but there was no immediate danger to him in the Philippines that we knew about. Apparently, he had become very disturbed when *The Inquirer* newspaper in Manila actually named him in connection with Robert Waldron's murder. I can only imagine that the DEA had arranged for Moynihan's smooth return home to England in return for his treachery. Also, money would have been involved somewhere along the line, that's for sure.

It was now 1988 and I decided to tidy things up and concentrate on my legitimate interests. A belated decision if ever there was one. Panache was legitimate but when the manageress offered to buy us out I quickly agreed. I had had a good run of three or more years and needed to focus on ToppFood and the manpower business. From a business angle, the selling of Panache was one of the more unusual management buyouts. I'm not sure whether any of the venture capital companies back at home would have touched it.

Although the alarm bells were ringing loudly, I decided I would finish the two deals that I had in transit and then pull away from the cannabis business once and for all. One was a consignment of grass bound for Australia, which I was setting up alone with Uncle Joe, and the other was with Howard and a bunch of others collecting and distributing the proceeds from a large consignment that was on its way into Canada.

The Canadian deal nearly proved fatal for me. There were 14 of us involved, which was stupid beyond belief. They never let the Royal family all travel on the same plane and similarly the major members of a drug network should not all decamp to the same hotel. It was a summit of investors in the deal and the purpose of the meet was to share out the spoils in a fair and orderly fashion, according to what had been agreed. Possession is nine-tenths of the law and the danger in not turning up was that a decision might be made, by committee, about your share of the proceeds.

I was feeling distinctly paranoid. Moynihan had spun. Had anyone else? I realised how stupid it was for us all to be in the one place and moved straight out of the hotel and into a flat. My fears were confirmed when I switched on the TV and heard of Canada's biggest ever drugs bust. I immediately caught a train from Vancouver to Toronto and then jumped on a flight back home to Bangkok. Regrettably I had no choice but to leave half a million dollars in a bag in the Vancouver flat. Someone got lucky. Later, the boys who had been collared unbelievably got bail and to a man they jumped it. Later still, one of our lads, Todd, got nicked in Atlantic City Casino by an undercover cop. They had him bang to rights; he was carrying US$4 million in notes in a suitcase. He had set up a deal with someone in the casino to launder the cash. They were offering him a better rate of return on his money than the traditional methods. This was no time to be taking risks. It was obvious that the DEA knew almost as much as we did. This was getting mad.

The really mad thing was that the load that was busted in Canada was not even ours! Our old mate Frederick was responsible for that one. Coincidentally the busted load was packed into crates bearing the print of a griffin or a condor-type bird. The police assumed the bird was a sparrowhawk (didn't they have a copy of the *Observer's Book of Birds*?) and that this was my trademark. They'd accuse me of sending an invoice next!

Howard and I had a meeting with Lord Moynihan. We couldn't resist it. If the situation weren't so serious, it would have been laughable. We just wanted to look him in the eye. To see for ourselves. Remember, we both liked him. Betrayal and treachery are hard things to accept, as the wronged partner in one in three of all marriages will testify.

'As a matter of interest, boys, what was the exact weight you sent into Canada?' He might as well have asked us for our air waybill numbers. He was bugging us and we fed him loads of shit but there was barely any pretence on either side. Neither of us would ever see Moynihan again.

Back at home I sat in my living room and looked at my girlfriend as I jigged my young daughter up and down on my lap. She was only three years old and I felt waves of guilt at the world I had brought her into. This was enough for me. I was rich. I had a loving and lovely family. I was not yet 40. With luck there was half a life to live. I wanted to live it. I felt so elated knowing that, after tomorrow, when I would be finalising my last ever hash deal in a downtown hotel with Uncle Joe – my Aussie colleague and good friend – my life would be a prosperous, contented, quiet one. It was coming on top but I only needed my luck to run for one more day – I'd be OK after tomorrow. I went to bed strangely exhilarated and liberated. I was about to go straight.

What I didn't know then was that the Amsterdam deal was not to be my last. The one before was.

Part Four

THE AFTERMATH

FROM MAHA CHAI TO THE BANGKOK HILTON – BANGKOK, THAILAND

Money had allowed me to get rid of my chains and won me some space to adjust to my new surroundings. Maha Chai had a bad reputation and I had heard tales of extreme brutality that had happened in this place but I never paid too much attention to them. People involved with drugs, whether their interest is recreational or business, tell stories like this – it's all part of the myth. I can remember when the Mods were doing battle with the Rockers on seafronts up and down Britain in the 1960s and you'd hear all these tales of Hell's Angels chopping people's arms off with axes. If this had really been the case, there would be a whole lot more 55 year olds nowadays trying to mow their lawns on a Sunday afternoon with great difficulty.

The most famous Maha Chai myth was the one about how the guards would put prisoners inside a bamboo-framed ball and roll them around the courtyard. Then they would lead an elephant into the yard and allow him to playfully kick the ball around with the terrified prisoner inside. Finally, when the elephant became bored, he would lift his huge foot and bring it down on the ball and the poor man inside. Everyone knew of someone who knew someone who had witnessed it but nobody had actually spoken to anyone who had witnessed it themselves. It may have happened in the old Siam centuries before, but so what? As a form of punishment it doesn't sound much worse than burning ugly women alive at the stake for being witches.

Because there was space and the opportunity to stretch one's legs and form relationships, I would say the prison was far more bearable than the Immigration Centre. It was not a happy place but certainly it did not stink of the same abject misery and bubbling despair. This is not to say that many of the people in this prison were not walking tragedies. Take Peter and Simon, for example.

I met Peter, a good-looking German man, early on when I strolled over to him in the yard and introduced myself. Peter was a con artist and had been living it up in Bangkok working stolen credit cards. One afternoon he stopped for a drink in a roadside bar and struck up a conversation with a young Englishman, Simon. Simon had married a young Thai girl he had met at college in England and was visiting her country for the first time.

After a couple more drinks, Peter went on his way but was arrested in a shop nearby when his stolen Diners Club card failed him. Peter knew he had problems. As I have mentioned earlier, the Thais take a harder line with economic crime than any other. He asked one of the policemen if he would take a note to a man in a nearby bar asking him to contact the German Embassy on his behalf. When the police got to the bar, Simon was still there. Unfortunately. His eyes were just a little bit glazed as he drank another beer and soaked up the bustling Bangkok street life around him. Soon he'd go back to the hotel and wait for his wife, who was visiting some old friends.

'You Simon?'

'That's right,' Simon replied, politely dismounting from his stool. The policemen promptly arrested him for being Peter's accomplice. Back at the station, Simon looked to Peter to iron out this misunderstanding and Peter tried. But Thailand is Thailand. They were remanded in separate custody and Simon remained convinced that he would be vindicated in court.

A month later they appeared before the judge. Peter pleaded

guilty and received a two-and-a-half-year sentence. He thanked the judge and took the opportunity to tell him that Simon was entirely innocent and they had met only an hour earlier in the bar. Ominously the judge did not even look up from his papers. Simon, understandably, pleaded not guilty. He *was* not guilty. Thai judges, though, do not go a lot on that. Someone really should have warned him. In Thailand, if you are a *falang* (foreigner) there is no concept of 'innocent until proved guilty' — it is 'guilty until paid otherwise'. He gave Simon five years. Peter eventually received a King's pardon and had his two and half reduced to one and a half but Simon, because he did not admit guilt, ended up doing the full five.

As in the Immigration Centre, the Chinese were busy trading openly. From hot water to heroin. From tobacco to toilet paper. In fact, they'd get almost anything you needed. It struck me as more than ironic that many of these people were banged up for dealing drugs, yet in here they were traded openly like packets of Persil in a supermarket. On occasions, though, a guard would snatch a joint from someone's mouth and demand money in exchange for not reporting you. As a non-drug user I did not have these problems. One of the saddest sights was to see men arrive and turn to heroin to ease their incarceration. It was bad enough to lose chunks of your life through your own folly but to re-emerge into the world as a heroin addict was tragic.

The Chinese really are an admirable race. They will make the best of whatever circumstances they find themselves in. They are natural traders and also natural gamblers. And like no other race, they can arrive in a foreign country and survive and prosper without putting anyone's nose out of joint, in fact often without anyone noticing. Every major city has a Chinatown that readily becomes part of the cultural fabric of that place. A place to visit. A place to enjoy. Contrast that with, say, Southall in England. In England in the 1950s and '60s, bigoted landlords put up signs in their windows proclaiming NO BLACKS, NO IRISH. Why not NO CHINESE? The Chinese have successfully integrated in practically every society in the world by not integrating. They come, they graft, they keep their heads down and they get on with their lives. Most crucially, they stick together. They adapt their lifestyles to the culture of the country they are in and get on with it. As long as they can celebrate Chinese New Year, care for their families and have access to a betting shop – they are happy. But cross them at your peril – in prison or out of prison. When world judgement day finally comes, whether it is nuclear, chemical or environmental, my money is on the Chinese being the last men standing.

As well as the junkies and the traders, there were the loonies. I'm sure they were like anyone else when they arrived but now they had taken to walking around the perimeter of the yard. Some pointed down at the ground as if counting, others had animated conversations with themselves and a few scoured every inch of ground for scraps and fag ends. One man with a long matted beard jumped around the yard, like Ben Gunn on acid, trying to catch cockroaches, which, when he was successful, he hungrily devoured. This is not as outrageous as it sounds because in Thailand the sane people eat cockroaches. They are considered a delicacy.

Now and then someone would make the serious error of upsetting the guards. The punishment I am about to describe may not be in the elephant foot on the head class but in terms of the damage done it was perhaps comparable. I saw it happen twice, possibly three times. Prisoners had their heads shaved and their pates completely painted with red oxide. They were then led out into the burning sun and chained up so they could not seek the shade, and over the course of the day their brains literally fried. Next time you saw them among the 1,800 inmates they would be plodding around the perimeter expressionless and silent.

Just as I was finding my feet, making friends, settling down and awaiting the outcomes of the various trials of the 'Howard Marks drugs ring' that were starting to take place and would give some pointers to my fate, I was moved again. Howard had been arrested at the same time as me at his home in Palma, on Majorca. Although he had resisted extradition to the US for a period, he was now in jail in America awaiting his trial.

Daniel Hamrogue, or 'Danel' as the Thais preferred to call me, was taken to Klong Prem Prison, known by those on the inside as The Bangkok Hilton. I was taken in an open-backed Toyota truck from prison to prison. Cyclists and pedestrians looked at me in my chains with a guard either side when we stopped at traffic lights on the road to Don Muang Airport. They were only vaguely interested. I was just another greedy, stupid European who was not going to see his folks for a long, long time.

Klong Prem is an imposing building with a large archway leading into a courtyard overlooked by two stern towers. The Japanese used it during the Second World War as a base when they paused for breath before moving over towards Burma. It was there that British prisoners of war were brutalised whilst building a railway, an episode that was immortalised in the film *The Bridge On The River Kwai*. The Japanese have never really left either. They are the biggest foreign investor in Thailand with brands such as Honda, Toyota and Suzuki clogging up the country's roads and streets and they still come over themselves in armies, but this time they have Nikon cameras hung around their necks instead of machine guns.

Next door to the men's prison was a women's prison. I wondered if there would be any communication. It was possible, I guessed: if the money was right. At the time I arrived, the women's prison housed one of the more famous people in Thailand. Her name was Mair Shamoi and she headed up a pyramid selling game that had swept the country a couple of years earlier. When it collapsed, as they always do, the papers claimed that there was more money tied up in it than there was in the entire Thai banking system. Mair's brother was in Klong Prem with me. Despite being demonised by the media in Thailand when everyone started losing their hard-earned Baht, her money almost brought Mair her freedom, as she would be allowed out during the day in her designer gear and return at night to keep up the pretence of serving a sentence.

History repeated itself on arrival when we went through the whole 'You Philip Sparrowhawk', 'No, me Daniel Hamrogue' game. The guards didn't really give a shit and soon started calling me Danel but first we had the ritual of a big fat Burmese trusty prisoner telling me to lie down whilst he clamped rusty elephant irons around my ankles.

'*Sip Haa*,' he puffed. I knew that meant 15. He was telling me that it was 15-kilo rusty chains he was bolting around my legs.

The guards showed a great deal of interest in me. First, my case (or Howard's case) had attracted huge publicity the world over and in that respect I was a celebrity. Second, I was the first man in the Thai prison system that the US had ever sought for extradition and third, they suspected I had access to money. A visitor from a laudable organisation called Prisoners Abroad told me that my extradition could take anything from six months to six years. The important thing as far as the Yanks were concerned was that I was not going anywhere. They would get around to me when they were good and ready. I hoped they never would if it meant serving time in the States. I preferred to be incarcerated here in Bangkok than America or even England. I did not have the problems with the culture and the people that some Europeans and Australians had and I knew that the American and British penal systems would be far less well disposed to bribery. There was no way I'd be able to get Kentucky Fried Chicken for 40 delivered to B Wing, Heathfield Road, Wandsworth.

A guard led me to my cell and I followed slowly behind, holding the strip of cloth tied around the middle of my chains to lift them from the floor and therefore enable me to shuffle. The chains started cutting into my ankles straight away. It wouldn't be long before all the skin would be scraped away and the mosquitoes would be laying their eggs in my open sores – I'd seen it before. A couple of boy helpers scurried alongside the guard and when I entered my cell they swarmed over me with long tailor's scissors and cut the bulk of my clothes away. I think they were looking for valuables. The cell had bedrolls for three and I sat back against the wall in my rags.

There was a 40-watt lightbulb in the ceiling that remained on day and night, a hole in the ground that served as a toilet and a trough and a tap screwed precariously into the wall. If this was the Bangkok Hilton, then these were the cheap rooms.

After a couple of hours my cellmates returned and introduced themselves. One was a polite young Englishman named Simon and the other an African-American called John. Simon was far more communicative and welcoming than John, who regarded me with outright suspicion. He behaved like I was a common thief and began attempting to hide his meagre belongings. Simon asked what I was in for and I gave them both a watered-down version. I tried to pitch myself somewhere in the middle of the truth, not wishing to give the impression of being some celebrity prisoner and big-time Charlie but on the other hand not coming across as a minion to be walked all over.

'And you?' I enquired of Simon.

'Well, you'll never believe this, Daniel, but I'm innocent. I know every single prisoner in the world thinks he is innocent but I really am. You see I was sitting in this bar in Bangkok and I got chatting to this German . . .'

'I believe you,' I interrupted. I was sharing a cell with the man that Peter the German had unwittingly condemned to a foreign prison. Small world. John wasn't so forthcoming but from what I could make out from his story he was a Vietnam War veteran who had somehow managed to perpetrate some large-scale frauds on US soldiers in Vietnam and Thailand.

In the morning, the key-boys scurried up and unlocked our door. Why they needed guards here was unclear – the lazy bastards got the boys to do everything whilst they lay on mattresses in their rooms watching TV and smoking. Their biggest exertion was to pocket some Baht for little extras provided to the prisoners. The whole prison system was centred on the golden rule that the guards must not have their routine disturbed in any way. Their routine being to do nothing all day long. Anything that forced them to veer from this was severely frowned upon. If you kept this golden rule, you'd survive. The Thais like their serenity and they like their holidays. Only Thailand could boast three New Year's Days.

Simon and John were in a hurry to get out into the yard, an open area the size of a football pitch surrounded by bamboo huts with banana leaf walls and roofs. Due to my chains I could not keep up with them. They went off to eat and I followed them in the direction of the huts; they seemed to be a hive of activity and as smoke was emitting from their chimneys I assumed that there was some cooking going on. I was fucking ravenous. In the first hut, a Spanish man sat sorting and reading mail, around him other prisoners sat or reclined on camp beds reading English, Thai and Spanish newspapers, while others were cooking eggs and rice. In the next hut I found Simon looking after some chickens for a German guy called Yamo. That was his job in here. Chicken bodyguard. Back in England he had been a marketing manager for a medical products company. Yamo, he told me, was very powerful in the prison. He was physically strong and prone to violence but had also converted to Islam which gave him an automatic status with the Arabs and the money some of them had access to. Simon noticed me practically fainting as the food cooked all around me on little stoves.

'Are you hungry?' Of course I was hungry. I would have eaten a scabby monkey but preferably one of Yamo's chickens who pecked at the ground around my feet. Simon passed me a bowl of rice. It was the best bowl of rice I have ever eaten. When I had finished, six seconds later, Simon took me to Harry's hut.

Harry was Chinese and his hut served as the general stores. It was known as the Coffee Shop. As far as shop proprietors go, he struck me as pretty miserable.

'Harry, this is Daniel.'

'So what?' Harry grunted.

'Well, Daniel has money.'

'Daniel, pleased to meet you.' His hand was outstretched and his lips retreated to reveal yellow and very loose teeth.

'Harry,' I smiled. 'I have money coming in shortly. Let me have some credit on some goods and I'll pay you back and pay you well.'

'How much money?'

'Enough.'

Harry agreed. Next I got Simon to take me to the Building Chief. Apparently he was the most powerful man in the prison after the Governor and Vice-Governor. He was certainly the most powerful guard on our block. He was laid back in his chair with his bare feet up on his desk and pulling hard on a cigarette.

'What do you want?'

'I would like the chains off, please. How much?'

He was very uninterested and there was a risk he would dismiss me. *'Nung Moon*?' I suggested. That meant ten thousand and I knew that would make him sit up.

'Ten thousand?' he repeated, just to ensure I knew my Thai.

'Fine. Can I have them off now please?'

'No. When you pay.'

'I have money coming in. I will pay. I want them off now.' Simon frowned at me; he was trying to relay the message that I shouldn't really talk to the Building Chief in this way. But he could see I was serious and that I would not be so mad as to welch on a debt to a guard (or anyone else) in a Thai prison.

One of the reasons I like Thailand and the Thai people so much is that their corruption is so open and so democratic. Unlike in Western countries – England and America spring to mind – it is not dressed up as anything else, and anyone can take part. In those other countries, and especially in England, the opportunities for corruption are prohibited from cascading down society's ladder. It's fine for town planners to take bribes, for ministers to accept 'loans' from wealthy individuals, for football managers to receive bungs, for prime ministers to encourage political donations and then dish out a gong in return. But should a prison warder be found in England selling a lump of puff, they'd jump on him and lock him up as well.

Free of my monstrous manacles I almost skipped back to Harry's with Simon following behind. He urged me not to rush.

'Never rush anywhere in here,' he wisely advised. 'The one thing we all have here is time. If you rush anywhere people will know you are up to something, a hundred hungry eyes will be on you.' I slowed down and joined the other people not rushing in the general direction of the Coffee Shop.

'Harry, I need 20,000 Baht.' Sitting behind Harry was an older Chinaman called Mr Lee, who I discovered was a bit of a face in the prison. A man not to cross, I was informed. Harry looked around at Lee and he nodded.

'Fifteen per cent charge is OK?'

'Is OK, Harry.'

I bought an exercise book from Harry and stuck 10,000 Baht in notes inside then headed back over to the Building Chief's office and handed him the book with the money just visible. Debt one was paid off. I was praying Pao wouldn't get run over by a bus or a tuk-tuk.

Simon was excited about my progress on this, my first morning. He took me to see Gamon, a screw with a bit of a power, who promised to build me my own hut for 15,000 Baht. They started on it that day. Finally I gave Simon some money to purchase some decent food to eat back in the cell, or room as Simon preferred to call it.

After a couple of days people were becoming curious about the Englishman who apparently had money. Walter, a charming American man, came and introduced himself to me. Walter and I had something in common as we had both had experience of a particularly nasty American DEA agent. Walter had been captured with seven tons of Thai sticks in the South China Sea. When the Yanks questioned him, he claimed an ounce was for his personal use and he had no idea how the rest had got there. The American agents are renowned for their lack of a sense of humour and this particular guy rammed his gun deep down Walter's throat. This same agent had waylaid Tony, my brother, in a Manila street, waved a gun under his nose and assured him that if he 'blew him away' now, nobody could do a thing and nobody would care. I was not surprised to hear from Walter that the guy had shot two Filipino officers dead when they had conducted a joint raid on a suspected drug dealer's house in Manila. The man was a menace, a bully and a psychopath. Sadly, law-enforcement agencies the world over attract this sort of nut. Thankfully he was asked to leave the Far East for good and his employers sensibly obliged because, as sure as Terry Wogan wears a wig, had he stayed around he would have been 'accidentally' shot by Filipino police.

Walter introduced me to some fellow Americans, Ken and Robert, both also in for Thai grass. I knew Walter was class when he asked me what product I was moving. Any smuggler of any note rarely used the word drug. It was always product or commodity and we didn't smuggle or peddle – we moved. We four in this hut were heavy-duty movers. The three Americans all lived in relative luxury and appeared to enjoy the support of the US Embassy. The Embassy, they assured me, had financed the building of their hut. The power of the United States of America is something to behold and even in here the Thais would have thought carefully before mistreating these people in any way.

Staff from the British Embassy visited regularly, especially a kind, canny and patient lady called Carol Downs, but there was little they could do for me, as officially I was still Irish. She knew I wasn't but formally I was still Daniel Hamrogue. He was no good to me now. I'd have to come clean and become Philip Sparrowhawk once more for the first time in many years. The Irish Embassy people came now and then but they were not stupid. They knew I was an imposter and were not going to waste time on me.

Strangely my American pals disliked John, my cellmate, but their countryman.

'He is a snake. He is with the Nigerians, not us,' they explained. Other than the fact that he was a bit moody (understandable, since he was locked up with a bunch of nutters on the other side of the world to home) I couldn't see what the problem was with him.

Unfortunately their dislike and mistrust of John was due to nothing other than good old-fashioned Yankee racism. Mind you, Walter distrusted Ken and urged me to do the same on the grounds that he was a born-again Christian.

'Worst of the lot, the born-agains. I'm sure they are a cover for something far more sinister,' he'd mutter.

The American race are as fucked up as the rest of us, despite setting themselves up as the incorruptible bastions of the new order: the upholders of truth, justice and equality. The dollar bill says it all – 'In God we trust'. Tough if you happen to be a Buddhist, Hindu or, God forbid, an atheist.

Walter also pointed out the AIDS corner. Their section behind the huts was a modern-day leper colony. Paranoia over the disease was building and these five or six poor souls received no interference from guards or inmates alike. They were fed, but no other human contact was attempted.

'There's a Yank and a Brit in there, Dan, but no one fucks with that lot,' Walter told me with unintended irony.

RUNNING THE SHOP
– BANGKOK, THAILAND

There was nothing wrong with the Nigerians in my book. They formed the biggest single non-Thai race in the prison and their numbers were growing rapidly. As they did not have access to money (this is the reason they were in here in the first place, as I will explain) they had to rely on their camaraderie and their physical strength to survive. Most of them stood over six foot in their sandals and were built like brick shit-houses. The Thai men on the other hand were often a foot smaller and slightly built. Physically there was no comparison, so the Thais did not ever seek confrontation. If they did, they knew the Nigerians would stick together. They had to.

I always found them surprisingly jovial, laughing heartily and flashing their white teeth at you in beaming smiles. This was surprising because at the hands of the white man, and in this case the white drugs traffickers, they had lost their liberty yet again. History repeating itself. These young men would be lured to places like Thailand where they would be offered $5,000 to smuggle through heroin on a Bangkok to New York flight. They were not criminals; in the country, tribal areas of Nigeria and other parts of Africa they came from, there were no laws to break. They had no concept of crime, punishment or prison, and $5,000, if they got it, was truly life-changing. The real crime though was that they were mere cannon fodder. The Americans paid them $2,500 before and

$2,500 on safe delivery. However, what they did not know was that they were stool pigeons for someone else, white and respectable, on the same plane who would be bringing in a quantity of smack ten times the amount the Nigerian was carrying. If anyone was going to be stopped and searched at Customs it would be the black Nigerian. Busted. To ensure he or she was stopped they'd make a tip-off phone call. Whilst he stood there in the Customs room with the sweat rolling down his neck, the white couple would sail through loaded up with packets of heroin. The drugs traffickers had lost $2,500 and a small amount of heroin on the Nigerian but had got through up to a quarter of a million dollars worth of heroin in one trip. The white couple would have got a nice few quid and the Nigerian would have got 25 years.

I got my hut. A nice detached des res with a south-facing garden. I spent my days reading week-old newspapers and chatting to other inmates. I soon became interminably bored and wondered what I could do to keep my brain active. I had a prison account with 50,000 Thai Baht credited to it and anything that was available in Klong Prem was within my grasp. However, any hopes I had of conjugal visits with Pao or liaisons with ladies from the women's block were soon dashed. It didn't happen. Visiting was a free-for-all where inmate and visitor stood six feet apart and shouted to one another but could not enter the no man's land between to talk and touch. The prison assigned me a job of making artificial flowers, which I suppose beat sewing mailbags, but I soon delegated this to another prisoner for the price of a packet of Krong Tip fags a day.

I made friends with a lovely English guy called Tom. He was the great-grandson of Lord Balfour and he had had a good job and been betrothed to an heir to the Scottish & Newcastle Breweries fortune. That was before he got nicked trying to smuggle heroin out of Bangkok Airport. He coped with his change of circumstances remarkably well and of course he had access to some cash but I worried about him as it was obvious he was not in good health.

Besides looking generally malnourished, his chest and arms were covered in large red sores and his skin was flaky and dry. When he offered me his hand for a good old hearty English handshake, I gripped only lightly in case his should fall off. His great-grandfather had been Prime Minister of Britain in the 1900s when he was already an old man. Before that he had earned the epithet 'Bloody Balfour' when he had been Chief Secretary for Ireland and had ordered soldiers to open fire on protestors who were agitating over Home Rule.

My brother sent me in a beer-making kit disguised as plum jam in jars and we had this busily fermenting away in my bamboo hut. These kits were all the rage in England for a while when I was a teenager and many a house had one of these things rigged up in the airing cupboard or under the stairs. I remember when mine became ready to drink it tasted rank and my dad and I had to throw it away in the garden. Over here we didn't care what it tasted like. It was alcohol and we loved every little droplet.

Christmas came and I had my first real bout of depression. The Americans were trying to extradite me and every few weeks I received visits from DEA people trying to get statements. I did not cooperate. I could not. I was Daniel Hamrogue not Philip Sparrowhawk. I wanted them to give up on me and leave me to the Thais, who I believed would not charge me with anything and let me go forthwith. That was my game plan. I had a Thai lawyer on my case, Napaon. He really believed in me and became passionate about winning my freedom. I'm not sure why, as he must have known I was as guilty as fuck.

That first Christmas I wrestled with it all, trying to keep my head above water. But I kept thinking about snow. It is weird what you miss, but the thought of snow caved me in. Snow on Epsom Downs. Snow outside my house. I imagined the boys having their Christmas Day drink in The Wellington on Epsom High Street, resplendent in their new Christmas-present pullovers and lining their stomachs with lager before the turkey, roast potatoes and gravy at home. I thought of Roy and wondered what he'd be doing at this moment. Actually I knew what he'd be doing. Shagging. Didn't matter where Roy was in the world he'd be at it. I missed his cheeky grin and sparkling eyes. I thought about the family in England and welled up. Shirley sprang into my mind and my guts twisted. Guilt stabbed me in the stomach as my mind drifted on to Pao and my baby daughter, totally innocent in all this. She thought she was getting involved with a soap powder whizz-kid and ended up with an imprisoned 'drugs baron'. How wise her parents now seemed.

On the boredom front, I got a break when the Chinese and the Nigerians went to war and there was the threat of the prison erupting into violence. The truth was I stage-managed the whole sequence of events. Not being a drug user, chess player or homosexual, my recreational interests were limited and I needed to keep my brain alive. I figured the only way to do this was by trading. I decided to stage a coup to take over Harry's Coffee Shop.

The Chinese and the Nigerians were at loggerheads and they had had a proper tear-up in the television room. The Nigerians were big and brawny but the Chinese were lithe and acrobatic. Those Bruce Lee scenes in *Enter the Dragon* were not as far off the mark as one might imagine. When it went off, they were flying through the air, jumping to great heights and kicking the Nigerians in the head whilst emitting high-pitched screams. Many broken bones and a few gallons of claret later, order was restored and honours were about even. Resentment, however, simmered. The Building Chief was worried. The Nigerian contingent in Klong Prem was growing all the time and the last thing the Thais wanted were full-scale riots. I went to see their leader, a guy we unimaginatively nicknamed Friday. He was a good, friendly and cheerful chap and he and I had already established a bit of a relationship. Their main beef was the deal they got from the Coffee Shop. Their orders were often unfulfilled and in terms of getting what they wanted they were always last in the queue. In prison what may appear to be a minor problem often takes on major proportions. In short they were fed up with being treated as second-class citizens. I asked Friday if they would be happy if I took over the Coffee Shop and he said they would be delighted. I suggested that the following day he should gather as many of his men together as he could and that they should mob up outside the shop menacingly but wait for me to act. This they did and, as I had expected, the Chinese began to gather menacingly too. The Building Chief became extremely anxious. I suggested to him that perhaps I should take over the Coffee Shop. He readily agreed and summoned Mr Lee, the leader of the Chinese. I did my best to make it seem like the idea had come from the Building Chief but Lee was not stupid. However, he was in no position to go against the Building Chief. I called Friday and the Nigerians off, and was installed there and then as the new proprietor of the Coffee Shop.

The Europeans were happy, the Thais were happy, the Americans were happy but the Chinese weren't. I was able to increase the product range and generally improve the shop's efficiency. There was not a problem with getting money out of the customers: the prisoners all had accounts and we held little cards that debited against these. I only extended credit to those people I was absolutely sure about. However, the Chinese boycotted the store and sourced their goods from the shop in another block which reduced the turnover substantially. As trading was their life and their chief instrument of power in this place, I knew that for the first time I had set myself up for a fall and started to watch my back.

My worst fears were realised when a petty incident almost turned into something far more serious and brought home to me the fact that, however much money I had access to, it could not buy me absolute safety. I was happily cutting up some fish outside the Coffee Shop when a scraggy Chinese youth came up and snatched one of the fish heads. Simon spotted it and grabbed the boy's arm, and I saw the boy reach over and pick up a knife off the table. People didn't pick up a weapon in this place unless they were going to use it. Instinctively I grabbed a piece of wood to clump him with, but, instead of lunging at Simon, he drove the blade straight into my side and ran away. It wasn't absolute agony but it was quite horrible. Being stabbed is the ultimate invasion of one's privacy. They say that one never quite gets over being burgled and the feeling of being violated. It was like that for me when I was stabbed. The physical pain was bearable but the thought of having a foreign object driven inside me was abhorrent and stays with me to this day. Fortunately, although I lost a great deal of blood, no serious damage was done internally and I was stitched together and was up and about as normal the following day. However, the incident snapped me out of the false sense of security I had been enjoying. The place was full of people on the edge. People who were mentally ill. People who harboured murderous thoughts. I should never forget that. The stabbing incident made me quite depressed.

As the summer came, my mood improved. One of my biggest strengths, I feel, is my temperament and it is that which has carried me through life and situations that might have sunk others. I try not to fret over what has passed and I refuse to worry over what hasn't happened yet. Therefore I only have to concern myself with the here and now and I'm a great one for making the most of whatever situation I find myself in. I do not understand people who waste energy hating, blaming, envying and regretting – it's all so negative and pointless.

The Chinese finally came round following my actions after I had been stabbed. The Building Chief summoned me and the boy in front of him and was quite clear that he believed the boy was guilty, I was innocent and that I could dictate, within reason, his punishment. Jumbo, a very influential Chinese man in the prison, but not a thug of any kind, had attended the meeting to represent the boy. I told the Building Chief that I wanted the boy to receive no punishment and that the incident should be forgotten. This went down well with Jumbo and he promptly broke the boycott by purchasing some oil drums from the stores from me. As word got around about this, the other Chinese followed suit.

The shop went on to become a great success. I was earning enough to buy a new cell on the ground floor with painted walls and functioning fan. The guards were earning and so were all the people around me. I had become the most influential, powerful and useful prisoner in our block. One evening I was approached in my cell by one of the blueboy trusties, who asked me if I would sell heroin in the stores on behalf of the Assistant Vice-Governor. He told me that 200 grams a week was the likely market in the prison and that the Vice-Governor would rather it was done by someone trustworthy and reliable and that it was only coming from one source. The addicts with money would get it one way or another and the Vice-Governor would rather it was coming from his sources and the revenue being earned therefore accruing to him. I felt I had little choice but to accept and I was assured there would be no comebacks to me. It was sold under the counter to existing addicts only; I would never have tried to convert new customers to this particular product. When my opening stock of 400 grams in a bag was delivered, I couldn't believe it. Outside, people would kill for one solitary gram.

The way that the junkies injected the heroin in there was by taking the refill tube of a biro pen, removing the ink from the tube and replacing it with heroin. They would then jab this into their vein, having to be very, very careful not to push in any air, as an air bubble in the vein could mean almost certain death. Some went this way. I was amazed at the size of the heroin market in the prison and with some early profits I purchased syringes from the hospital wing and at least made their habit a little safer. The Vice-Governor was delighted with the concentration of the trade and he gave me a pass that allowed me access to anywhere in the prison except, of course, the front door. Throughout all this, I could never get my head around the fact that I was talking to people all day long who were doing ten years or more for being caught with various quantities of heroin on their person and I was carrying twice that amount in my back pocket. The world was mad. The world is mad.

I don't know what it was about the upper classes and Klong Prem but I was always coming across people whose ancestors had been prime minister, or heirs to old British fortunes and the like. I'm not sure where Eddie fitted in the British class system but he did have a good old double-barrelled name. Eddie had been caught doing travellers' cheques. It was a simple scam. You got chatting to a tourist and when you felt you could trust them, you'd offer to buy some or all of their travellers' cheques. You gave them between 25 and 50 per cent of their face value. They'd go off to the nearest police station and report them as stolen and then Thomas Cook would replace them at full value under the holiday insurance. Meanwhile you'd go and load up on goods on the cheques before their serial numbers were circulated. It was easy small-fry fare but the problem was that if you were caught, the Thai courts dished out a year for every $100 travellers' cheque worked. Eddie was caught and got 11 years. He passed the time playing chess.

The unpredictability of the law in Thailand worked both ways. There was yet another well-to-do Brit in with us called Carl, if I remember right. He had murdered his Thai girlfriend and was serving 18 years. Without any warning, the King of Thailand, who was celebrating his 65th birthday, declared that all grandfathers would be released from Thai prisons. Bye bye Carl.

Now I was running the Coffee Shop and managing the drug supply, the guards treated me with much respect. The prison had become a tranquil and well-ordered place and the Vice-Governor at least was making plenty of money from the habits of his guests. I was making plenty too and this was a valuable safeguard for me. I was under no illusion that my relatively easy life was due to anything other than money. Not muscle. Not connections. Just cash. If my source should be cut off for any reason, I would be as vulnerable as the next man. Should anything happen to Pao I would be in trouble.

The guards asked me to help them with all sorts of things: besides selling drugs and general supplies I was asked to find an English language tutor for the Vice-Governor, help dispose of dead bodies and most memorably look after three *katoeys*.

These three lady-boys had come from various parts of the prison and their respective guards were complaining that the prisoners could not work with them around and they were unwittingly causing unrest. I could see why. All three possessed glistening long black hair, breasts and pretty faces with pouting lips. It was hard to remember they were male. What on earth was I to do with them? Tom promptly christened them Nik, Nak and Noo, as a play on the word NickyNackyNoo, but when I asked him what that meant he did not know. I later found out how they ended up in Klong Prem. Nik – or was it Nak? Maybe it was Noo. One of them had gone off with a punter who had badly beaten him/her up. He/she came to the bar the following day badly battered and bruised. Later that night the same punter turned up. He was English and probably believed his ten quid bought him violence as well as sex. More likely he was disgusted with himself for shagging a girl with a dick. Whatever, the male inside these girls wanted revenge and they waylaid the tourist up a back street and smashed his head in with a metal bar.

Simon was shocked when he walked into the hut and met them for the first time as they lay around looking decorative. He took it in his stride. He really was the perfect English gentleman abroad. Noel Coward would have been proud of him. Simon was straight. Remember he was the one who really should not have been there in the first place, and he showed no signs of temptation, but Walter, the racist faggot-hater, was a different kettle of fish.

'Well, well, well, and who are these lovely ladies?' he asked, his eyes working up and down their bodies.

'The Three Degrees,' I said.

'Nik, Nak and Noo,' Simon explained. 'They are boys, Walter.'

Walter said he knew that and assured me that he had no interest in shagging them.

'A blow job maybe,' he added, poking his tongue into the inside of his cheek. From that very first day Walter sort of adopted them. He said, with some justification, that they were easy on the eye and good company in comparison to most of the men in the prison.

'But they *are* men, Walter, don't forget that,' I implored.

'Well, sort of,' Walter agreed.

'Walter, if you put your hand inside their shorts don't be surprised if they have cocks bigger than your own.'

'That won't be difficult,' replied Walter with his endearing self-deprecating humour.

He was right: Nik, Nak and Noo were good company. In an all-male environment something even remotely resembling a woman was welcome. The fact was that these three more than remotely resembled women. Except for the genitalia they were women. They chatted like girls, giggled like girls, moved like girls and smelt like girls. Simon, Walter and I felt as protective towards them as we would have done towards girls on the outside. The problem for Simon and me at least (and possibly Walter – we'll never know) was that they wanted to have sex. So did we – but not with them. It would be the start of a slippery slope. They started to have sex with various prisoners and this made them much happier. We weren't overly happy about it but it kept the peace. We tried to vet their customers as we really didn't want them catching AIDS, but it was hard. Nice as they were, Nik, Nak and Noo defined themselves through sex.

One of the many peculiar practices that Klong Prem agreed to was the visits from bands of hippies. They visited whatever embassy they fancied and, armed with a list of prisoners, would come and visit us. Essentially we had become a tourist attraction made fashionable by films like *Midnight Express*, but the hippies kidded themselves and us it was some sort of brotherhood thing. The family of the weed showing solidarity and all that. I would go along when called because you never knew, you might just meet someone interesting and anything to break up the routine was welcome.

Normally I'd be sitting opposite some boring old fart with a silly Jesus beard who wanted to talk about someone called Nick Drake. Walter had it sussed, though, he'd home in on the pretty young hippy girls and 'connect' as quickly as he could. He'd start to tell them about how hard it was to remain heterosexual in this environment and if only she would lift up her top and show him her tits it would keep him on the straight and narrow for the foreseeable future. You'd be surprised how many did.

One day, after two years of living the life of a favoured prisoner, I walked past the Governor's house and stood and faced it as I bowed. This we were taught to do, just as we knew to stand for the national anthem. It may sound odd now but it wasn't so long ago that us boys had to bolt out of the Epsom Odeon cinema before the end of the film so we could avoid the national anthem. It used to come on at the end of the film and the entire audience would stand as it went on and on. It was not done to leave while it was playing but we wanted to nip next door to The Marquis of Granby in time for last orders. This is why my generation doesn't know the end of any British films between 1955 and 1970. Did Michael Caine die in the end in *Zulu*?

Close to the Governor's house was the Vice-Governor's office and, being nosey, I peered inside. Two men were sitting, deep in conversation. One was Phil Matthews, Head of Customs at the British Embassy, and the other I guessed was DEA. He was Mexican-looking, wearing black Ray-Bans and chewing like he had overindulged on amphetamine. When he saw me staring in at them, he exploded.

'What the fuck is he doing here? Why isn't he under lock and key? The motherfucker should be in solitary.' He jumped from his chair and ran out of the office to lunge at me but Phil Matthews and a guard held him back. I really was taken aback by the violence and rage of the man. Why did the Americans take this so personally? That was the difference between the British authorities and the Americans. The Brits knew it was a game. We won some, they won some. There were never any hard feelings. With the Americans it was all so very personal. Like you had raided their personal bank account or worse still had been caught interfering with their children.

Phil Matthews followed me as I wandered off.

'Sorry about that, Phil. He's very quick-tempered,' he said. There was no point in pursuing the Daniel Hamrogue shit with him. They knew exactly who I was. He had a photo album full of pictures of me, my house in Thailand, my dad's house in England, my driving licence and all sorts of other stuff.

'Who is that prick?' I asked.

'He's a leading DEA special agent. It's his life's work to nail you, Howard and the rest. He wants you bad in the States. You don't do yourself any favours walking around here like you own the place – he wants you to suffer. If he thought you already were, he'd be content to leave you here. But I'm afraid that's not going to happen. He's going to take you back to America, Phil, if it kills him.'

I wished someone would. In my heart I knew Phil Matthews was right. He didn't like being pushed around by the DEA any more than me, but the Americans called the tune. If they wanted their man, they simply went in and got him. Extreme examples of this are their invasion of Panama to get President Manuel Noreiga and, more recently, Iraq to do Saddam Hussein.

Sure enough this agent and his cronies stepped up the pressure and it soon became a regular occurrence for me to be manacled by the hands and the feet and taken in a fast car to the local courthouse to resist extradition proceedings. It wasn't until my 21st such trip that my case actually got heard in front of a judge. All the other times, other prisoners were heard before me and they didn't quite get around to us. I wasn't complaining. When I finally clanked up the wooden stairs to stand before three bewigged judges, I feared the worst. If you were in chains and you were in front of them, as far as they were concerned you were guilty.

Napaon, my highly committed lawyer, stood up and explained I was opposing my forced extradition to America.

'Why should we stop them?' enquired one judge.

'Because Thailand does not have an extradition treaty with the United States of America for one,' replied Napaon. That foxed them. The senior judge dismissed the case.

I was elated, but Napaon warned me that the Americans were unlikely to leave it at that. I knew it too, but at least I was proving a tough nut to crack and my time out of America was being extended.

Sure enough, some months later, Napaon and I were back in front of the judges. This time the American representative produced a leather folder with the American eagle embossed in gold on the front and presented it to the bench. They opened it up, read the letter inside and passed the folder between them. They kept running their hands over the leather and tracing the eagle with their fingers, reading the letter over and over again. They were like awestruck kids at Christmas. I don't know what the letter was or who it was from but I can guess. I reckon that the zealous DEA agent had got President George Bush the First himself to pen a note to these judges to ensure my extradition. I can think of nothing else that would have had such a stupefying effect on them. They upheld the extradition application.

Napaon launched into an emotive speech about how my human rights were being violated and how, more importantly, Thai law was being breached and undermined and they were allowing imperial political motivations to interfere with their legal process. To my amazement he started crying before them. They didn't like this. As I have said before, the Thais do not like confrontation, whether it be physical or emotional.

'Do not behave like this in our court or we will hold you in breach,' ordered the senior judge.

After we were dismissed and I was told I was going back to Klong Prem whilst my transport to America was arranged, I put my arm around Napaon but he was inconsolable. My fight against extradition was over.

BACK IN THE USSA
– MIAMI AND SEATTLE, USA

Back in Klong Prem I managed to get to speak to Phil Matthews from the British Embassy. Suddenly being extradited to Britain seemed attractive to me. But, as Phil rightly pointed out, as soon as I touched down at Heathrow they (the US Government, FBI, CIA, RICO, call them what you will) would whisk me straight off to the States. It wasn't only the little countries the USA could push around.

It was about this time I received a letter from Lord Moynihan. Its very arrival caused much excitement in the prison. The blueboys came running into my hut one afternoon. They were shouting and yelling, 'Danel, Danel, the Vice-Governor wants you now.'

I wondered what I could have done wrong. The boys were behaving like headless chickens although headless chickens would not be able to speak and, come to think of it, would be unlikely to speak English if they could. Being summoned before the Vice-Governor was the same as being summoned before the Governor. All officials in Thailand delegate their jobs to the person below them. The Governor was rarely seen inside the prison walls.

The Vice-Governor welcomed me into his office and was pleased that I spoke a few words in Thai to him. I thought maybe he was concerned about me going to America with my knowledge of the drug set-up in Klong Prem. But no, he handed me a letter that bore the House of Lords crest and was sealed with red wax.

'You have important letter.'

He told me to go back to my cell and read it; I couldn't believe they hadn't opened it. I think he thought it was from the Prime Minister or even the Queen. I opened it in front of him, tucked the unread letter in my pocket and handed him the envelope. He was over the moon at this small gift. Little did he know that the letter was from one of the biggest crooks with blue blood that England has ever known.

It was a strange letter from Moynihan. It was postmarked London for one. So I figured it was part of his deal to be able to return home. He was trying to justify his reasons for assisting the British and American police in convicting us. He claimed that Howard had seduced his wife when she had visited Hong Kong. If this was true, I could understand that he'd be upset, but I certainly hadn't had my wicked way with his missus so why did I have to be dragged into it? I doubted it were true anyway. Howard had never shown the slightest interest in any of the Mrs Moynihans. I found out, years later, that about this time Moynihan had visited England and had tried to repair some family issues and tie up some loose ends. I was obviously one of those loose ends.

Six weeks later the guards came and told me that I had to collect my belongings because I was on my way back to the Immigration Centre pending my imminent deportation. I said a fond but quick farewell to my friends. The stores would have to go under new management. Tesco should take a look – the money we were taking. Me, Simon, Robert, Walter, John, Friday, Tom and the others had been together for three years and had become close. 'Should I Stay or Should I Go' by The Clash blared out of Simon's transistor radio. Unfortunately, I had no fucking choice in the matter. As I signed some papers in the guards' office they were more interested in the new TV phenomenon than me. A strange yellow character muttering 'Eat my shorts' appeared to be transfixing them as he filled the screen.

Saying goodbye to Pao was tortuous. Her industry, determination and love had kept me going in the Thai jail system. In fact, it was her presence on the outside that kept many of us going. It is not only me that has a lot to thank her for. As well as missing her unconditional love, I was frightened to go to America without her.

But at our last meeting we were philosophical. Being in Thailand was limbo; in America we would get 'closure', as the Americans like to say, whatever that may have been.

Back in the Immigration Centre nothing had changed much. It had been four years since I had first arrived and they still had the overcrowding problem. Staggeringly, there were four or five people who remembered me and I remembered them. How they had survived in this fish tank was beyond me. Thankfully, I was fetched a day or two later by my favourite DEA agent himself and driven with an over-the-top escort to the airport. There was no need for him to come and collect me himself, but this was his time. We had had ours. Now the fun really began. Turning down my request to pop into the duty-free shop, they hustled me through to a boarding gate and on to an overnight flight to San Francisco, stopping at Tokyo en route for refuelling. At San Francisco there was no time to put flowers in our hair or anywhere else because I was bundled straight on to an internal flight to Miami. From Miami Airport it was off in a people-carrier down to the M.C.C. State Prison in Dade County.

This is real Dukes of Hazzard territory. There are not many branches on the family tree around these parts. This is the home of the tobacco-chewing redneck, the cattle rustler and the Ku Klux Klan member. The locals would string a black man up from a tree here if they could still get away with it and the menfolk are nearly as bigoted. The prison is in the middle of nowhere. Very Paul Newman in *Cool Hand Luke*. Guards armed with shotguns look down on you in their Ray-Ban shades from watchtowers and razor wire encloses the 20-foot-high fences. We went through a series of gates and electric fences before being taken into a reception area in the inner sanctum. This is where I had my first strip search in an American prison. You stand in front of them bollock naked and they ruffle your hair first to see if anything drops out. In my case it was only congealed dandruff. Then you pull your lips up for them, then lips down, tongue up, tongue down. Lift your balls, lift your feet. Bend down and spread the cheeks of your arse. As I did this I couldn't help but get a vision of the redneck in the film *Deliverance* squeaking and screaming 'Squeal like a pig' as he gleefully buggered the lost tourist he had tied up to a tree. Fortunately they didn't touch but just had a good old look up my rusty old bullet hole. I have experienced no greater feeling of vulnerability than being forced to adopt that position and it was something prisoners were obliged to go along with time and time again. (Sometimes I pondered on the American preoccupation with arseholes. Along with 'motherfucker', 'asshole' is their favourite term of abuse, people down on their luck are 'bums' and at the first opportunity they are looked up by anyone in authority. Why is this?)

After this performance I was taken to a single cell where I was given a meal of burger and chips and a glass of a tepid orange drink they had the cheek to call Kool-Aid. After three days in the single cell, where they taught me to make my bed and how my sheets and pillow should be positioned, I was told I had now been acclimatised and was ready for entry to the main prison through another set of gates and fences.

The main prison consisted of four blocks surrounding a stinking old pond in the centre. I was put in a cell in one of the blocks, a two-storey building containing countless rooms, and told to wait. There were three beds but my new cellmates were obviously elsewhere in the prison. By now I had been issued with an identity card that I had to carry with me at all times. It had my photograph on it and at last my name was Philip Sparrowhawk again. The biggest difference between this jail and a Thai one, on first impressions, was the regimentation and the cleanliness. You seemed to be forever stepping over cons on all-fours mopping floors and cleaning walls. The smell of bleach was the dominant one. Orders were barked. Screws had straight backs and marched everywhere, arms swinging.

A white American called Keith was the first to arrive back at the cell some three or four hours after my arrival. He offered me the top bunk. Keith was in for dope smuggling too, explaining that he had a legitimate fishing business in Bermuda but the temptation to bring in dope from Jamaica by boat had proved too strong. He asked me about my case and I started to tell him.

'Crazy Phil. Wadda small world. Your buddy Howard, he was in here with me up to about 18 months back. I know all about your case. Well, I'll be damned. What a great fella he is, old Howard. Good man, Howard. One funny man.'

He was well and truly in the Howard Marks fan club was Keith. He filled me in on the prison and how to survive. Keep your head down. Don't mix with the wrong people. Nothing new there.

In the morning we were awoken by a loud fire alarm bell at six and had to wash, dress and make the bed before standing to attention facing the door. Then the doors were unlocked and we were marched down to the food hall where Rice Krispies, milk, eggs and bacon and a mug of tea awaited us. The food was good. The best I'd had now in four or five years. We sat six to a table and devoured our breakfasts in silence. I literally kept my head down as there were some mean-looking fuckers sitting around me. Many of the men were large with over-developed arm muscles and fingers like Harris pork sausages. I was determined to slip under their radar. After breakfast we were locked down again until eight when everyone was led off to their respective jobs. I was assigned gardening duties, which consisted of raking over flowerbeds that had been raked over the previous day and fishing bits of weed and algae out of the lovely pond. This was a short, sharp shock regime, except in my case at least it was likely to be a long, sharp shock.

There was a group of six African-Americans who walked around together and remained aloof from almost everybody else in the prison. The other cons were shit-scared of them. They were part of some religious fundamentalist group whose leader was one Jaweh Ben Jaweh but they also operated business on the outside. The redneck screws hated them because they were in for some particularly violent killings that had ended in their victim's heads being removed. I guessed that the victims must have been white; if they had been black the rednecks would not have cared. One day I got chatting to one of their group and we became friendly. I was just about the only con, black or white, who would sit and talk with them.

Most of the other blacks liked to work in the kitchens, where they were adept at making hooch from fruit and sugar. Ingeniously they managed to fill the fire extinguishers outside the cells with it and as we passed we were able to take a little squirt in our mouths as if we were passing the water fountain in our local park.

In my early days at Dade County I received a letter from an American lawyer that sent me mentally spiralling downward for a few weeks. This man had originally approached me in Klong Prem and had offered to take over my case after Napaon. He said he would work behind the scenes back in the States and that when I was finally deported he would appeal immediately for my release. Over those months he assured me things were going well and that he was cutting through the red tape. His final diagnosis was that I would be freed because 'it was clear they had nothing on me whatsoever'. The letter I received in Dade, however, was short and to the point. He could no longer represent me because of a 'conflict of interests'. The conflict I suspect was that, now I was in America, I could not arrange for lumps of cash to be delivered to his offices. I could see now that I'd been had. He was the criminal justice equivalent of an ambulance-chasing solicitor and he had milked me for just under one million dollars. He had probably not lifted a finger on my behalf. Stupidly I had pinned a lot of hope on this man and now he had dumped me. The problem in prison, wherever you are, is that you have only two things to clutch at: your penis and straws.

Worse still for me was that the DEA had kept themselves very busy identifying and sequestrating my assets. The papers said they had confiscated some $30 million, mainly cash, stored in bank accounts around the world. I did not realise I had that much but I always found the accrual of interest a pleasant surprise. I learnt later that the precise amount they identified and seized was $29,768,100. I wonder what happened to it? Technically, now I was skint. I started to regret all those bags full of cash I had left under beds and in hotel rooms and started to rack my brains for bank accounts I had opened in dodgy names and forgotten about. I also considered for the first time the likelihood of being repaid debts by people I had lent and given substantial sums to. The problem is that when you are down, you are down. Not many people are going to pay back $100,000 to a man they think they will never see again and is likely to rot in a prison for the next quarter of a century. I'd been here before but I was back with a vengeance. I did not have a pot to piss in. Actually, I did. It was in the corner of my cell.

Next thing, they sent in a legal aid girl to represent me.

'Hi, Philip, I've been assigned to your case,' she drawled as she flicked open a notepad and began to scribble with her pencil.

'Now, how much did they bust you with at Miami Airport?'

I looked at her in amazement.

'I wasn't busted at Miami Airport.'

'No? Where were you busted?'

'I wasn't busted anywhere. I have been extradited from Thailand after spending nearly four years in prison there.'

The silly, jumped-up little bitch hadn't even done me the courtesy of reading the case paperwork.

She came back a few days later suitably chastened.

'Philip, I'm very sorry but I will not be able to defend you. There is a file of over 8,000 pages on your case. It would use up our entire legal aid budget just to photocopy it. We just can't do it.'

'Who can?'

She remained silent. No one wanted to touch it — not on legal aid anyway. In a fit of pique I wrote to the trial judge and announced that I had dispensed of my lawyers and was now representing myself.

I even wrote to Mother Teresa, opening up with 'I don't know if you remember me but I met you on a flight some years ago and made a donation to your work in Calcutta . . . I have found myself in this predicament . . . I wonder if there are any strings you can pull.'

'Dear Philip,' she replied (fortunately she did not remember I was Daniel then — or was it Brian?), 'I have written to your judge as you have asked. But remember Jesus has already forgiven you', or words to that effect. Yes, but would Jesus give me a pardon?

One morning as I set off to work, two screws came and grabbed my arms, clamped handcuffs on me and shoved me into a punishment cell.

'We'll teach you to think about breaking out,' they sneered.

Breaking out? I could break out in a sweat as I raked over that soil but that was about it. I knew they were putting me in 'the hole'. I'd heard other prisoners talk about it, there was even a song they sang, '30 Days in the Hole'.

'Who sang that?' I once asked of one of them, a fearsome-looking, tattooed Hell's Angel gang leader who looked naked without his German Army helmet and Iron Cross.

'That was a great American live band called Humble Pie. You know 'em in England?'

Yes, I knew of them. They were English actually, fronted by Steve Marriott, formerly of The Small Faces and Peter Frampton of The Herd, but I decided not to correct him.

The hole had no natural light, an aluminum bed with no pillow and a piss pot. Nothing else. I tried to work out why they would throw me in here. There was no way I was breaking out or even thinking of breaking out and there was no way that the authorities could really believe I was. Was it because I was socialising with the Jaweh Ben Jaweh? Was my court case imminent and the DEA wanted to break my spirit? I had no idea. I was in for three days before being let out without any explanation. Another of life's little mysteries. While I was in the hole, though, I got talking to a guy in the cell next to mine. Obviously we could not see one another but we could shout to each other. I had heard him talking and cursing to himself. He spoke a very poor broken English and sounded South American.

'What are you in for, mate?' I asked.

'I am a political prisoner,' he replied, or that was the gist of it.

Once he started I could not stop him jabbering. I was in the hole with no less than the former President of Panama, Manuel Noriega. A bored guard sometimes translated his rantings to me. The US

Government suspected him of harbouring drug traffickers and in typical US style unleashed their full military might and invaded his country and overthrew his Government. I remembered all this at the time but hadn't paid too much attention; I certainly didn't know they had brought Noriega back with them and locked him up in a hick prison. And throwing him in the hole? That's no way to treat a statesman, surely? And if I thought I was a victim of US hypocrisy and conspiracies, I had nothing on this bloke. President Bush had set him up, he claimed. The CIA destroyed him. They wanted his country for control of the Panama Canal. It went on and on for hours. When they let me out, I was selfishly hoping they'd keep him in.

Shortly after this surreal interlude I was taken downtown to a place called the Igloo, where I met my prosecutor for my upcoming trial. He told me that I was going to get 25 years for importation and there was no point in fighting it. 'The average age of the jury will be 67 years old,' he said, 'and they'll convict you, no sweat.'

'How can I admit to something I didn't do?' I asked him. That day I was whisked across town to appear in the courthouse for some legal formalities. Things were hotting up again. In the courthouse I was locked in a room with a rather troubled guy who told me he'd been hauled in on a trumped-up rape charge.

'They're only going for me because I'm a Kennedy,' he moaned. Turned out he was William Kennedy Smith, a nephew of Senator Teddy Kennedy, himself a younger brother of JFK, and he'd been accused in the so-called Palm Beach rape case. I followed his case after that brief encounter and he was finally acquitted just before Christmas of 1991.

Back in prison I received a letter from Howard Marks. He started off by saying that I should plead guilty and tell the DEA anything they want to know. 'We have,' he wrote. I know you fucking have, I thought. He'd got 25 years at his trial but was hopeful of having that commuted considerably earlier. My feelings about Howard were ambiguous. He may have dropped me in it. He may not have. His attitude was, when the chips are down, you fight for yourself. Howard made that clear from the start and, let's be honest, I never went into anything with my eyes closed. I had always been the architect of my own destiny. However, when I turned the page of his letter I fell back in love with the Welsh bastard. His legal team (he had one – I didn't) had advised him that, due to a subtle change in law, if I pleaded guilty there was a strong chance that I would only receive time served, on account of the years I had already spent in foreign jails. Howard was urging me to do this for my sake. The others up on the same indictment as Howard and myself had all received time served. This meant the time they had served in prison awaiting the trial and during the trial was sufficient. They could walk free.

It was a gamble, a massive gamble, but I decided to go for it. I weighed it all up – there was no way I was going to get more than Howard. The worst-case scenario I figured was that I'd get about 20 years and possibly only 15. If they credited my time served at foreign year for US year then I'd get 15, possibly 10. With good behaviour I could be out in 10, possibly 7. That was my downside. From a gambler's point of view, the argument to follow Howard's advice was pretty compelling. I could not see any ulterior motive Howard could have in urging me to take this course.

The day I stood in front of Judge Paine and pleaded guilty, my heart was in my mouth and I kept my lips firmly shut because I felt physically sick. Rationalising is fine but there was always a small chance that this judge could decide I was the root of all evil, that I had corrupted Howard Marks and the rest of Western society and that I must be locked away forever.

'How do you plead?'

'Guilty as charged your honour.'

Short pause. I can't remember his preamble but the long and the short of it was, '16 years'. Smiles spread over the DEA men's faces. I'm still waiting. Long pause. I want to cry.

'But in the light of the time you have served both here and in foreign jails I am sentencing you to time served.' I do cry a tiny bit. The whole end-game process in the court took 30 minutes.

WELCOME HOME
– LONDON, ENGLAND

There were still some silly hoops to jump through. I thought that once the momentum had started building it would all be quick and easy. But I did not leave the court a free man. I was taken back to Dade, where in the morning I was re-arrested for entering the country illegally and dragged off to an airforce base on the outskirts of Miami. Then I was put on a clapped-out old war plane which the Yanks had probably confiscated from some tinpot country for making bagels without a licence, and flown to Seattle and a prison for illegal immigrants. I did not protest. I knew that some people have to maintain their face somehow.

The plane took me, in my orange prison jumpsuit and chains, and some guards to another airbase where we collected more prisoners and then 14 hours later on to Salt Lake City. This airline is affectionately known as ConAir. After the obligatory strip search and arse excavation we spent the night in a prison there. In the morning we were given a sandwich and a Kool-Aid and loaded on to a bus. From there we travelled for six days by road from prison to prison before finally arriving at Kent County Jail, Seattle. On the surface the place seemed far more relaxed. It was downtown with only 25 cells and the longest-serving con had done six months. It was full of parking felons and there was none of this 'Come here, boy. Do this, boy.' From the corridor window we could see a real American high street with real shops and real people.

After a few days a couple of guards picked me up in a people-carrier to take me to the main immigration prison. They were pleasant and chatty.

'Where you from?'

I listed the last few prisons I had stayed at.

'No, not what prison are you from. Where do you come from?'

I explained I was English but had been extradited after living for many years in Thailand. At the mention of Thailand their attitudes changed.

'As soon as we reach the prison we are calling a doctor for you, sir.'

'Why?'

'In case you have AIDS.'

'I haven't got AIDS.'

'Have you been to Vietnam?'

'Yes.'

'Well that is a country where AIDS is prevalent and as such we have reason to believe you could be carrying the virus. If you come near us or touch us, you are threatening us with a deadly weapon and you will be charged with threatening a guard.'

These blokes were serious and genuinely scared. They pointed me towards a cell and then produced a long pole and laid it on the floor. If I came further than the end of the pole, that would constitute an attack on them. Six days this went on, with the ridiculous charade of my cell door being opened, the pole being dragged towards them and then my dinner plate being pushed along the ground with it. This was 1992 and, in the American penal system, they were convinced you could catch AIDS just by touching someone. No wonder this lot insisted on looking up my arse. They were worried that the devil himself might live up there.

My blood test came back negative. That was positive for me and I was allowed entry into the main prison, which was a melting pot of blacks, Chinese and Hispanics. Besides the guards, I was one of the few white people in the entire place. I did three months in

Seattle and by now I was getting twitchy again. What was going on? Were they waiting on some new information to bring new charges? Had I just been forgotten or were they winding me up? Was the DEA more powerful than the judiciary? Finally, I was taken downtown to a court where the ridiculous charge of entering the United States of America illegally was read out.

'I did not enter here illegally. Your Government brought me here. I was extradited,' I pleaded.

'Well, it does not alter the fact that you entered this country without a valid passport,' concluded the judge 'I therefore sentence you to three months' imprisonment. Take him away.'

These Yanks really are not the full shilling. The following morning I was processed again and two guards took me off in a people-carrier. Where now? Alaska? Hawaii? They wouldn't tell me but they took my handcuffs off and were both smiling. One of them was the crank who thought I had AIDS.

'Do you fancy some Kentucky Fried Chicken?' said the AIDS man as he screeched up outside a dog-eared cardboard cut-out of Colonel Sanders.

From there they drove straight to Seattle Airport and out among the jumbos. I knew now what was happening. Planes were being loaded and unloaded. Small vehicles with orange flashing lights wove in and out of the loading bays. My guards pulled up alongside the rear door of a 747 displaying the British Airways logo. At this moment the world's favourite airline was most certainly mine.

'Here you go, Phil,' said the guard, 'you're going home.' They went to shake my hand and pat my back but both stopped short. Just in case. But they did stand on the tarmac and wave as I dreamily climbed the steps into the plane. A man in a suit with a delicious English accent asked me to sign some papers and then a stewardess sat me down in a first-class seat.

'Where are we going?' I asked.

'First stop, Heathrow.'

The other passengers stared at me. It's not often they are joined in first class by a bloke with no hand luggage, who does not know where the flight is going and is dressed in an orange jumpsuit and moccasins.

My hostess looked after me well, plying me with food and drink and providing a copy of *The Times* to read. There was a new Prime Minister: John Major was staring out at me. Where did he come from? Worcester Park, as it happens, just down the road from Epsom. He was not far off my age either. He was a working-class boy made good. I was a working-class boy made bad.

My mind turned to what awaited me at Heathrow. Would I be arrested on arrival? The Yanks had had their piece of me – maybe the reason they allowed me to go so easily (I had been there less than a year in total) was because they knew I was going to have the book thrown at me at home.

I fell into a deep sleep for much of the 14-hour flight, helped by copious amounts of red wine. As we began our descent into Heathrow the hostess woke me and I looked out of my window. I could see the Thames snaking across London, an image that I would see time and time again in the future on the opening credits of the TV soap *EastEnders*. Then, it was a programme I had never seen. It is something I don't regret missing the first ten years of.

I felt warm and emotional. It had been a long time. When we taxied to our stopping point, the other passengers sprang up and gathered their hand luggage and headed through the terminal to passport control. I had no baggage, and no passport come to that. Nobody was telling me anything and I was just left to my own devices.

As I approached passport control, I hesitated. BRITISH AND EU NATIONALS said one sign. DIPLOMATIC PASSPORTS AND OTHER said another. That's me. I'm OTHER. I was the only person approaching this particular desk. A tall man in a shirt and tie looked at the orange apparition approaching him. Behind him, but not with him, stood another big man in a suit.

'I'm British but I don't have a passport,' I announced.

'Philip?' The man behind stepped forward. I nodded.

'I'm Terry Burke. I was head of operations in tracking you down.'

'Thanks a lot.' He grinned and I grinned. He was from New Scotland Yard and I had seen his name in my case documentation. This was the first time we had met.

'I'm glad you are back safely. At some stage we'll need to have a chat. In the meantime, keep your nose clean.'

I was a free man. It was a lovely moment.

'Terry, can I ask you something?'

'Of course, what?'

'I need to get back to Epsom. I've no money. Could you lend me a tenner?'

I got on the tube to Victoria, where I noticed the London Underground rolling stock had been replaced or refurbished. On the concourse at Victoria Station an electronic noticeboard flashed in place of the old brown wooden slat contraption and bars selling cappuccino and baguettes had sprung up all over, replacing metal Nestlé vending machines. It had only been about ten years but it felt like a lifetime. The crowds of commuters stood and stared up at the noticeboard. I joined them and could see the Epsom train was in and waiting, but I didn't move. In the US prisons you didn't move until ordered to. I had to force myself to walk away from the throng. Other commuters threatened and frightened me as they barged past to jump on their train. In prison, physical contact was by express consent only. I am sure it had always been like this on Victoria station but I was out of practice.

I was in my 40s now. Middle-aged if I was lucky enough to make 86 years old. Old if I didn't. On the train to Epsom, the view from the window was almost unrecognisable. If you commute daily, you don't notice this creeping change to our urban landscape, but where had the old black windmill without sails gone that stood on the railway bank near Clapham Junction for centuries? What was with all these Sainsbury and Tesco red-brick castles? I was shocked. At Epsom I ran down the stairs leading down from the platform and out on to the concourse area. I was excited. Phil was home. Phil was back.

Coming into the station and hurrying over to the booking office was a familiar face. Mickey Dixon, my old school pal, who was with me when I won on Nijinsky over 20 years before when this whole ridiculous roller-coaster ride began. I probably hadn't seen him for ten years. Last I heard he was working behind the bar in The Wellington pub. He was in an overcoat and a fag wobbled in his lips as he paid the booking clerk. I was still in my orange jumpsuit.

'Hello, Mickey,' I said quietly, my whole body tingling with anticipation.

Mickey turned around and smiled, 'All right, Phil. How are you, mate? Look, can't stop, my train is due. Catch you later.'

He didn't even know I'd been away.

There was a black cab idling outside and I thought about getting in and asking him to take me up to Dad's on the Wells estate but I had no idea what the fare would be. It would surely be more than I had in my jumpsuit pocket so I decided to walk. I crossed the road and walked down the pathway that used to run behind the Odeon cinema, but the picture house was now gone. Yet another lovely old building that had been demolished to make way for the House of Sainsbury.

I emerged into Epsom High Street and was taken aback at the changes that had taken place in a decade. I had to stand still a moment just to absorb it. The traffic flowed just one way now. Lester Bowden, the gentlemen's outfitters that had been there as long as Epsom itself, had turned into a Waterstone's bookshop. The Spread Eagle pub had turned into Lester Bowden. The Lloyds Bank was now Lloyds TSB. The TSB was now nothing. Shops with names I had never heard of had sprung up. Cashpoints had proliferated. Restaurants and café bars abounded. The old green buses had turned red. Only the old red-brick clock tower stood there resolute among all this change and as I looked over at it, something else that refused to succumb to the march of time stood at a burger van below it, sipping at a plastic cup of coffee. Someone else, actually. There was no mistaking him as he his head turned back and forth, his eyes locked on to the bottoms and breasts of housewives as they bustled past him on their way in and out of the new Ashley Shopping Centre.

Unlike Mickey, Roy was excited to see me. He knew where I had been and, looking at my attire, he sized up the situation immediately.

'Phil, old son. You're out.' He beamed as his arms wrapped around my shoulders and he squeezed me into him, Eric and Ernie style.

'You look great,' he lied. 'So you dodged the electric chair then?'

'Just about.'

'I meant to come out and see you a few times. But you know how it is.'

'I know, Roy.'

'I've been doing great, Phil. I've been all over the fucking world. Haven't stopped mate. You know, ducking and diving,' Roy said, moving on to his favourite subject – himself. 'Had a spot of bother in Hong Kong. I'll tell you about that later. Great time in Oz. Look Phil, I'm going back there in a couple of weeks. I've got a real interesting opportunity out there. Come with me and I'll tell you all about it.'

'Are you serious?'

'Of course I'm serious, Phil. I've got this bloke on the inside, at the airport. I could get a herd of elephants through, I'm telling you.'

'Roy,' I said, stopping him mid-flow.

'What?'

'Fuck off.'

EPILOGUE
– HEAVEN, HELL AND EARTH

The Actor still acts. Because the BBC destroyed almost all of its pre-1970 archives he does not benefit from UK Gold repeat fees.

Gay Andy died in Thailand some years ago now from AIDS.

Bean is still in the music business and still playing the odd gig. The comeback has eluded him but he was never a man to succumb to the chicken-in-a-basket circuit.

Terry Burke called me up to his office at New Scotland Yard for a chat. He advised me to keep my nose clean. I polish it every morning. Last I heard he had a nice post looking into money laundering in Bermuda, the West Indies and the Cayman Islands.

Dad died in 1999 after spending his final years living with my family and me.

Danny inherited a Seattle bank from his father. Being a chippy, and not knowing what to do with a bank, he flogged it. He now spends his time building for love and not money.

Dave managed to forget who I was and avoid being tarred with my brush. He now has homes in England and Thailand.

The over-zealous **DEA agent** may have died. Howard told me this, so it could be wishful thinking.

Roy Dean lives well in Portugal. Sometimes he flies into England; I tend to fly out then to Thailand.

Mickey Dixon sadly died in 2002.

Uncle Ernie died in 2002 at 96 years of age. For a man who warned me against women, he managed to remain sexually active until his 87th year.

The Footballer managed to put his prison sentence and the whole sorry episode behind him and resume the decent law-abiding life he had previously led.

Frederick and his girlfriend were shot dead whilst shopping in the Philippines in 1994. I noticed recently that there is a Nina and Frederick tribute act on the European cabaret circuit. Not everyone reads the papers. They should be careful.

Friday was transferred only this year from Klong Prem Prison to Kefti Prison in his native Nigeria. He was the last man from my time to remain in the Thai jail. He is hopeful that when his case is reviewed he will be released. So am I.

James Ghana is working for the Red Cross in his native country.

Jason leads a blameless life having a pint and a bet in Wolverhampton.

President Ferdinand Marcos reluctantly abdicated in 1986. He died after some years in exile in Hawaii. His son Bong Bong has been fighting a case against his father's estate brought by a Filipino locksmith Rogelio Roxas who claims he discovered one of the gold Buddahs only to have his house raided by Marcos's men and the Buddah and its contents confiscated. A US court has ordered the Marcos estate to pay $22 billion. Bong Bong says he hasn't got it.

Howard Marks now has the celebrity he always craved and has been officially rebranded as Mr Nice. He was released in 1995 after doing seven years of his sentence. He has published books, toured with a one-man show and has become a key campaigner in the movement to legalise cannabis.

Phil Matthews is one of the heads of the UK Customs Investigations Department.

Ronald Milhench still hangs around the Philippines with his boat and his girls.

Mona remains a beautiful lady and oversees one of the finest massage parlours in Manila.

Lord Moynihan died in the Philippines in 1991 from a brain haemorrage. That's the official line anyway. His brother, former sports minister Colin, fought for his title to pass to him and he now sits (with his legs dangling) in the House of Lords.

Ruangsak Muangmulchair, Chief of Klong Prem Central Prison was moved to an inactive post at the Corrections Department following allegations of involvement in drugs and corruption. In June 2003 the *Bangkok Post* reported he was accused of conspiring with warders and prisoners to sell illicit drugs inside the prison.

Tim Munday lives in Japan but thinks nobody knows that.

Napaon was so devastated at losing my fight against extradition from Thailand he abandoned his career in the legal profession. He now runs a successful hotel near Bangkok.

Nijinsky was shot dead at the Kentucky Claireborne Stud in May 1992. He had reached a good age.

President Manuel Noreiga still resides in the US prison system. Possibly he is still in the hole.

Lester Piggott was knighted by the Queen and then promptly incarcerated on tax charges. One day I hope to meet up with him and exchange Derby and prison anecdotes.

P.J. Proby toured the UK recently with The Searchers. This was his first UK tour since 1965.

Shirley has a school secretarial post in the south of England.

Simon served his full sentence and now runs a casino in Russia. His Thai wife did not stand by him. He refuses to join Peter the German for a reunion drink.

Uncle Joe Smith was recently collared walking on to a yacht with A$5 million in his briefcase. He got ten years – a daunting prospect for a man the wrong side of seventy.

Philip Sparrowhawk married Pao and lives quietly in Surrey with his wife and daughter. Occasionally he unfurls a map of the Philippines with a big cross marked on it.

Sue lives quietly and happily in Australia with her family. Each night she thanks God she got out when she did.

Mother Teresa reached a grand old age but died a few years back. Her work continues though through her charities and she is due to be made a saint.

Todd enjoyed himself in prison so much he has made Thailand his home.

Tom was a model prisoner, confessed his guilt and remorse regularly and duly had his sentence commuted. He's now living quietly in Wandsworth, London.

Tony is retired, living and riding horses on his nice farm.

Walter served his time and now indulges his hobby of sailing.

Wanchai was never involved in any skullduggery and continued to build ToppFood into a thriving company. They now employ some 260 people. Somehow I reckon I've been erased from the corporate history page in the annual report.

Jack 'The Fibber' Warren died an old man in Australia last year. His legend in his home country is growing and I heard a film of his life is being made.

FURTHER READING

ON CANNABIS

Cannabis: A History, Martin Booth, Doubleday, London, 2003

ON HOWARD MARKS

Mr Nice, Howard Marks, Minvera, London, 1997
Hunting Marco Polo, Paul Eddy and Sara Walden, Little Brown, London, 1991

ON GROWING UP IN EPSOM

Common People, Martin Knight, Mainstream Publishing, Edinburgh, 2000

ON THAILAND

The Damage Done, Warren Fellows, Mainstream Publishing, Edinburgh, 1998
Thailand, Joe Cummings and Steven Martin, Lonely Planet, London, 2001

INDEX